THE NEW STRONG-WILLED CHILD

Workbook

DR. JAMES DOBSON.

TYNDALE™
MOMENTUM

An Imprint of
Tyndale House Publishers, Inc.

Visit Tyndale online at www.tyndale.com.

TYNDALE is a registered trademark of Tyndale House Publishers, Inc. *Tyndale Momentum* and the Tyndale Momentum logo are trademarks of Tyndale House Publishers, Inc. Tyndale Momentum is an imprint of Tyndale House Publishers, Inc.

The New Strong-Willed Child Workbook

Designed by Dean H. Renninger and Alyssa Force

The material in this workbook has been adapted from *The New Strong-Willed Child.* Copyright © 2004 by James Dobson. Published by Tyndale House Publishers. Workbook questions written by John Perrodin.

All Scripture quotations, unless otherwise indicated, are taken from the Holy Bible, *New International Version,*® *NIV.*® Copyright © 1973, 1978, 1984 by Biblica, Inc.™ Used by permission of Zondervan. All rights reserved worldwide. www.zondervan.com.

Scripture quotations marked KJV are taken from the *Holy Bible,* King James Version.

Scripture quotations marked NASB are taken from the New American Standard Bible,® copyright © 1960, 1962, 1963, 1968, 1971, 1972, 1973, 1975, 1977 by The Lockman Foundation. Used by permission.

Scripture quotations marked *Phillips* are taken from *The New Testament in Modern English* by J. B. Phillips, copyright © J. B. Phillips 1958, 1959, 1960, 1972. All rights reserved.

Scripture quotations marked RSV are taken from the Revised Standard Version of the Bible, copyright © 1946, 1952, 1971 by the Division of Christian Education of the National Council of the Churches of Christ in the United States of America. Used by permission. All rights reserved.

Produced with the assistance of The Livingstone Corporation (www.LivingstoneCorporation.com). Project staff includes Dave Veerman, Betsy Schmitt, and Andy Culbertson.

ISBN 978-1-4143-0382-6

Printed in the United States of America

16   15   14   13   12
8   7   6   5   4

CONTENTS

INTRODUCTION

At times do you find yourself thinking, *I love this kid more than anything in the world, but I don't really like him or her very much. We can't get along for more than ten minutes without clashing over relatively insignificant matters. Why does this child make me so angry, when what I want most is harmony and love? Why is our relationship so unsatisfying and disturbing? What did I do to mess up something that began with such promise and hope? Not only have I failed my child, I have failed God, too.*

The New Strong-Willed Child was written for frustrated, discouraged, and confused parents like you. Dr. Dobson wants to put an arm around moms and dads who are struggling in this most important responsibility in life. You wanted to be a perfect parent, doing that job with greater success than any other. Instead, it now looks as though every good intention has been misinterpreted, resented, and resisted. Is that where you are today?

Parenthood can be a guilt-inducing proposition. Babies often come into our lives when we are young and immature, and we have no instruction manuals to guide our first halting steps. No manufacturing tag comes attached to a newborn's wrist that says, "Some assembly required." So we take these tiny human beings home with us, not yet knowing who they are, and then proceed to bumble along as best we can. As a consequence, many of the day-by-day decisions we make on their behalf are the result of sheer guesswork, as we hope against hope that we are doing the right thing. Our own inadequacies also get in the way. We become tired and frustrated and selfish, which sometimes affects our judgment.

In those moments, we react without thinking and realize the next morning that we handled things all wrong. In short, children are so maddeningly complex that it is impossible to raise them without making many blunders and mistakes.

As parents, we are given the privilege of taking the raw materials that comprise a brand-new human being and then molding that child, day by day, into a mature, disciplined, productive, and God-fearing adult who will someday live in eternity. Doing that job right, despite its setbacks and disappointments, is one of life's greatest achievements.

Loving those we have borne *is* a risky business but also one that brings great joy and happiness. Even though trials and tears often accompany the challenge, the journey is noble.

Dr. Dobson hopes that when your offspring are grown, you may "have no greater joy than to hear that [your] children are walking in the truth" (3 John 4).

1

THE WILD & WOOLLY WILL

GETTING IT STARTED

Who's in charge here?

Children want to know how tough their leaders are. They respect those who show power and courage. Thus, whether you are a parent, a grandparent, a Scout leader, a bus driver, or a schoolteacher, sooner or later one of the children under your authority will clench his little fist and take you on. You had better be prepared to prove him wrong in that moment or the challenge will happen again and again.

Dr. Dobson calls this defiant game "Challenge the Chief," and it can be played with surprising skill by very young children. He tells the story of a father who took his three-year-old daughter to a basketball game. The child was, of course, interested in everything in the gym except the athletic contest. Dad permitted her to roam free and climb on the bleachers, but he set definite limits regarding how far she could stray. He took her by the hand and walked with her to a stripe painted on the gym floor.

"You can play all around the building, Janie, but don't go past this line," he instructed her. He had no sooner returned to his seat than the toddler scurried in the direction of the forbidden territory. She stopped at the border for a moment, then flashed a grin over her shoulder

1

to her father, and deliberately placed one foot over the line as if to say, "Whatcha gonna do about it?" Virtually every parent the world over has been asked the same question at one time or another.

The entire human race is afflicted with the same tendency toward willful defiance that this three-year-old exhibited. Her behavior in the gym is not so different from the folly of Adam and Eve in the Garden of Eden. God had told them they could eat anything in the Garden except the forbidden fruit (in effect, "Do not go past this line"). Yet they challenged the authority of the Almighty by deliberately disobeying His commandment.

Perhaps this tendency toward self-will is the essence of original sin that has infiltrated the human family. This is why proper, immediate response to willful defiance during childhood is required, for that rebellion can plant the seeds of future personal disaster. The weed that grows from it may become a tangled briar patch during the troubled days of adolescence.

BEFORE YOU BEGIN

1. Describe a time when you (the parent or teacher) won the "Challenge the Chief" game. Then recall a time when your child was the victor. What made the difference?

   _____

   _____

   _____

   _____

2. Why do you think children need borders and boundaries?

   _____

   _____

   _____

   _____

3. How can a strong will be a negative trait? a positive one?

_____

_____

_____

_____

4. How do kids treat leaders they don't respect?

_____

_____

_____

_____

5. When you were a child, how would your parents have described you?

_____

_____

_____

_____

LAYING IT OUT

NO TURNING BACK; NO BACKING DOWN

Really, you don't understand.

Unless you've had a strong-willed child of your own, you can't comprehend the unique challenges such parents face.

When a parent doesn't stand up to his or her child's defiant challenge, though, something changes in the relationship. The youngster begins to look at his mother and father with disrespect; they are unworthy of his allegiance. More important, she wonders why they would let her do something so harmful if they really loved her. The ultimate paradox of childhood is that boys and girls want to be led by their parents but insist that their mothers and fathers earn the right to lead them.

LEARNING FROM BAD EXAMPLES

Dr. Dobson tells the story of a certain little spitfire. At thirty-six months, he had already bewildered and overwhelmed his mother. The contest of wills was over. He had won it. His sassy talk—to his mother and anyone else who got in his way—was legendary in the neighborhood. Then one day he rode his tricycle down the driveway and into the street, which panicked his mother. The woman rushed out of the house and caught up with her son as he pedaled down the street. She took hold of his handlebars to redirect him, and he came unglued.

"Get your dirty hands off my tricycle!" he screamed. His eyes were squinted in fury. The woman did as she was told. The life of her child was in danger, yet this mother did not have the courage to make him obey her. He continued to ride down the street while she trailed along behind, hoping for the best.

How could a tiny little boy at three years of age buffalo his thirty-year-old mother in this way? Clearly, she had no idea how to manage him. He was simply tougher than she—and they both knew it. This mild-mannered woman had produced an iron-willed youngster who was willing to fight with anyone who tried to rein him in, and you can be sure that his mom's physical and emotional resources were continually drained by his antics.

SOME KIDS HAVE CROOKED WHEELS

In thinking about the characteristics of compliant and defiant children, Dr. Dobson sought an illustration to explain the vastly differing thrusts of human temperaments. He found an appropriate analogy in a supermarket. Here's how he describes it:

> Imagine yourself in a grocery store, pushing a cart up the aisle. You give the basket a small shove, and it glides at least nine feet out in front and then comes to a gradual stop. You walk along happily tossing in the soup and ketchup and loaves of bread. Grocery shopping is such an easy task, for even when the cart is burdened with goods, it can be directed with one finger.

But buying groceries is not always so blissful. On other occasions, you select a cart that ominously awaits your arrival at the front of the market. When you push the stupid thing forward, it tears off to the left and knocks over a stack of bottles. Refusing to be outmuscled by an empty cart, you throw all your weight behind the handle, fighting desperately to keep the ship on course. It seems to have a mind of its own. You are trying to do the same shopping assignment that you accomplished with ease the week before, but the job feels more like combat duty today. You are exhausted by the time you herd the contumacious cart toward the checkout counter.

What is the difference between the two shopping baskets? Obviously, one has straight, well-oiled wheels that go where they are guided. The other has crooked, bent wheels that refuse to yield.

Do you get the point? We might as well face it: some kids have crooked wheels! They do not want to go where they are led, because their own inclinations take them in other directions. Furthermore, the parent who is pushing the cart must expend seven times the energy to make it move, compared with the parent of a child with straight wheels. Of course, only mothers and fathers of strong-willed children will fully comprehend the meaning of this example.

THE CLASSIC STRONG-WILLED CHILD

How is the strength of the will distributed among children? Dr. Dobson originally assumed that this aspect of human temperament was represented by a typical bell-shaped curve. He presumed that a relatively small number of very compliant kids appeared at one end of the continuum and an equally small number of defiant youngsters were represented at the other. The rest, comprising the majority, were likely to fall somewhere near the middle of the distribution. However, having talked to at least 100,000 harried parents, Dr. Dobson is now convinced that his supposition was wrong.

Dr. Dobson, however, warns not to take this observation too literally. Maybe it only *seems* that the majority of toddlers are confirmed anarchists. Furthermore, there is a related phenomenon regarding sibling relationships. In a family with two children, one is likely to be compliant and the other defiant. Who knows why it works out that way? There they are, born to the same parents, but as different as though they came from different planets. One cuddles to your embrace, and the

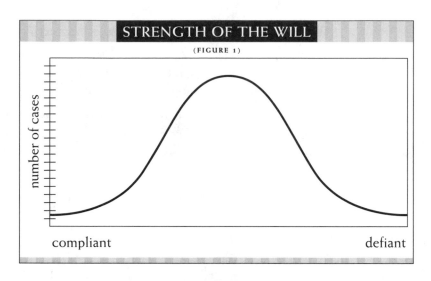

STRENGTH OF THE WILL
(FIGURE 1)

number of cases

compliant   defiant

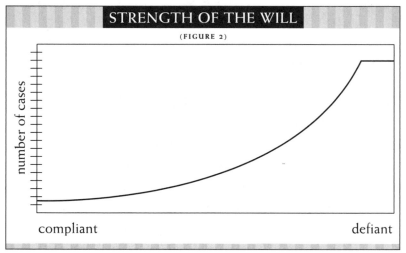

STRENGTH OF THE WILL
(FIGURE 2)

number of cases

compliant   defiant

other kicks you in the navel. One is a natural sweetheart, and the other goes through life like hot lava. One follows orders, and the other gives them. Quite obviously, they are marching to a different set of drums.

DEFINING THE COMPLIANT CHILD

The compliant child is not necessarily wimpy or spineless. That fact is important to our understanding of his nature and how he differs from his strong-willed sibling. The distinction between the two is not a matter of confidence, willingness to take risks, sparkling personalities, or other desirable characteristics. Rather, the issue under consideration here is focused on the strength of the will—on the inclination of some children to resist authority and determine their own course, as compared with those who are willing to be led. Dr. Dobson believes that these temperaments are prepackaged before birth and do not have to be cultivated or encouraged. They will make themselves known soon enough.

Your child may not fit either pattern. Another category of temperaments in children includes those who are not really strong-willed—at least, their assertiveness is not expressed in the same way. The distinction here is not one of independence and aggressiveness. It is a matter of tactics. They rarely challenge the authority of their parents or teachers in a stiff-necked manner, but they are willful nonetheless. Dr. Dobson calls them "sneaky."

Adults think these youngsters are going along with the program, but inside, subversion is afoot. When no one is looking, these children break the rules and push the limits. When caught, as inevitably they are, they may lie or rationalize or seek to hide the evidence. The appropriate approach to these sneaky kids is not appreciably different from handling the strong-willed child. Sooner or later, his or her self-will can be expected to break into the open, usually during early adolescence. Then, it's "Katie, bar the door."

THINKING IT THROUGH

1. In what ways is parenting what you expected? How does it differ from what you expected, especially regarding your children's temperaments?

_____

_____

_____

_____

2. When have you felt guilt, self-condemnation, or self-doubt in your parenting?

_____

_____

_____

_____

3. When have you felt that others were judging you for having a strong-willed child, especially other parents who have compliant children?

_____

_____

_____

_____

4. Do you believe everything will work out for the best for your strong-willed child? Why or why not?

_____

_____

_____

_____

5. Why do many parents fear being firm with their children?

_____

_____

_____

_____

6. How do you respond to parents whose children are obviously out of control? How do you respond to "helpful comments" from your friends or family members?

_____

_____

_____

_____

7. If it is true that a child is strong-willed from birth, what are the signs? What might be the signs for a compliant child?

_____

_____

_____

CASE STUDY:
Portrait of an Angel

Consider the following case study of a strong-willed child from Dr. Dobson's files:

Dana slept through the night at maybe fifteen months old. At eighteen months old, you could tell her no and she would fall on the floor, throw a fit, and roll around. We would sit and watch her for a while because we weren't going to give in. We were going to be strong. She would stand up, and she would have that beautiful angelic face, and she would say, "I'm sorry."

She would come over and lay her head in my lap, and then she would bite me. That was the first clue because it was a manipulation. She made sure that you weren't worried about what she was going to do, and then she would bite. She was very, very tough.

Later, there was an episode where she had been out throwing rocks at cars. I called her in and I said, "Dana, why were you throwing rocks at cars?" She said, "Well, I did warn them. I told them they didn't belong on my street. As they went down the road I told them if they came back by, that I'd have to throw a rock at their car. So I threw rocks at them." I took her in to spank her and she said, "You're not going to spank me. I'm going to wait until my daddy gets home."

She knew the longer she could put off a spanking, the longer she had to work up her defense. I said, "No, I'm going to spank you now." She said, "No, you're not. You will not spank me." I said, "Yes, I will." That day, I think, was a terrifying day because I physically could not control her. She threw every ounce of strength and determination into fighting me. It was a battle that probably lasted an hour and a half—and this child was five years old. It ended with my putting her out in the garage. She was walking around screaming.

Then she rang the doorbell, and she said, "I'll take my spanking now." I did spank her, because I knew if I ever let her win one of those battles, I would never have control of her again. But it was a constant struggle.

When Dana was in her first year in college, she wrote this note in midyear:

Dear Mom,

Hey there. This is going to be a weird letter. I've been doing a lot of lifelong thinking. Mom, sometimes I wonder where I would be and what life would be like if I hadn't come back from the dark side. You know, I never thought that I would consider my mother to be my best friend, but you are. I would never trade this closeness I've gained with you for anything in the world.

You and Dad used to say that if I would just wait until it was time for me to move out, that you would be behind me 100 percent. Now I understand. I know that you and I were growing, even when I was at home, but I don't think that I ever truly appreciated you until now. At least, not as much as you deserve to be *appreciated. I miss you every day. I mean, I thought that when I went to school I would never want to go home or even call. But I don't like to go through the day without talking to you.*

You know, I hope that one day I will be as successful as Daddy. I want to be as keen and respected in my field as he is in his. But you, above all, had the hardest profession of all. You had to raise me. Mom, I hope that you understand what a gift God gave you. He gave you the will and the power to raise me. You showed me the kinds of things that no college or professional school could ever teach me. I can only pray that one day God will make me the kind of mother you have been and will always be to me. I just wanted to take a minute to say, "Thank you" and "I love you."

Your baby girl,
Dana

POINTS TO PONDER

1. Do you think Dana's parents should have responded to her differently? What would you have done in their situation?

2. How have you and your spouse resolved the issue of spanking?

3. We know that not every story has a happy ending. How would you deal with a strong-willed adult?

_____

_____

_____

_____

4. What would it mean to you to one day receive a letter like Joy did from her daughter Dana?

_____

_____

_____

_____

DIGGING DEEPER

JACOB AND HIS CHILDREN

Read Genesis 37:1-11 focusing on verses 3, 4, and 11.

[1]Jacob lived in the land where his father had stayed, the land of Canaan. [2]This is the account of Jacob. Joseph, a young man of seventeen, was tending the flocks with his brothers, the sons of Bilhah and the sons of Zilpah, his father's wives, and he brought their father a bad report about them. [3]Now Israel loved Joseph more than any of his other sons, because

he had been born to him in his old age; and he made a richly orna-
mented robe for him. [4]When his brothers saw that their father loved him
more than any of them, they hated him and could not speak a kind word
to him. [5]Joseph had a dream, and when he told it to his brothers, they
hated him all the more. [6]He said to them, "Listen to this dream I had:
[7]We were binding sheaves of grain out in the field when suddenly my
sheaf rose and stood upright, while your sheaves gathered around mine
and bowed down to it." [8]His brothers said to him, "Do you intend to
reign over us? Will you actually rule us?" And they hated him all the
more because of his dream and what he had said. [9]Then he had another
dream, and he told it to his brothers. "Listen," he said, "I had another
dream, and this time the sun and moon and eleven stars were bowing
down to me." [10]When he told his father as well as his brothers, his father
rebuked him and said, "What is this dream you had? Will your mother
and I and your brothers actually come and bow down to the ground
before you?" [11]His brothers were jealous of him, but his father kept the
matter in mind.

Clearly, Jacob loved Joseph best. This story explores part of the damage done by
favoring one child over another.

1. If someone outside your family observed you, would he or she say that you
   have a favorite among your children?

---

2. If you conclude that you have both a strong-willed child and a compliant child, how will you ensure that you don't favor the one who seems to consistently behave better?

_____

_____

_____

3. How can you show each child that he or she is precious and loved?

_____

_____

_____

TAKING IT HOME

Dr. Dobson offers two helpful observations for parents who are raising strong-willed children. First, he says, it is common for these moms and dads to feel great guilt and self-condemnation. They are trying so hard to be good parents, but the struggle for control at home, day after day, leaves them frustrated and fatigued. No one told them that parenthood would be this difficult, and they blame themselves for the tension that arises.

They had planned to be such loving and effective parents, reading fairy tales by the fireplace to their pajama-clad angels, who would then toddle happily off to bed. The difference between life as it is and life as it ought to be is distressing.

Second, Dr. Dobson writes, it is important to realize that parents of strong-willed children face unique challenges. All too often, parents of compliant children don't understand their friends with defiant youngsters. They intensify guilt and embarrassment by implying, *If you would raise your kids the way I do mine, you wouldn't be having those awful problems.* Willful children can be difficult to manage even when parents handle their responsibilities with great skill and dedication.

POINTS TO PONDER

1. Come up with a list of examples of strong-willed adults, either family members or famous individuals. What traits do they have in common? Which of those characteristics do you see in your children?

2. When have you experienced guilt about your child's seemingly wild behavior in a store or restaurant? How could you better convey the need for boundaries outside the home? What do others expect of you and your strong-willed child?

3. Create profiles for your children. Do any of them fit the classic strong-willed child profile? Do any of them fit the compliant child profile? Are any of them what Dr. Dobson would call "sneaky"?

_____

_____

_____

JOURNALING

1. Talk about your fears with God in prayer. Share your longings and desires for your strong-willed child. Write out a prayer that God will use _____'s strength for His glory.

_____

_____

_____

2. Describe areas in your child's (or children's) life that are especially in need of prayer.

_____

_____

_____

3. What would you say (if you could say anything) to the parents of "model" children to help them understand the unique trials of raising a strong-willed child?

_____

_____

_____

_____

4. Record some of your recent failures and victories as a parent.

_____

_____

_____

_____

5. Write out your dreams for your child, taking into account his or her strong-willed nature.

_____

_____

_____

_____

2

STRONG EVIDENCE ABOUT STRONG-WILLED KIDS

Taken from chapter 3, "What Makes Them the Way They Are?"

GETTING IT STARTED

COLD HARD STATS

What do we know about children with particularly strong wills? That question has intrigued Dr. Dobson for years. Very little has been written about these youngsters, almost no research on which to base an understanding. Dr. Dobson sought to change that and conducted a survey of thirty-five thousand parents to learn what their experiences have been. Here is a summary of his findings.

★ There are nearly three times as many strong-willed kids as those who are compliant. Nearly every family with multiple children has at least one who wants to run things. Male strong-willed children outnumber females by about 5 percent, and female compliant children outnumber males by about 6 percent. Thus, there is a slight tendency for males to have tougher temperaments and for females to be more compliant, but this can be, and often is, reversed.

★ Most parents know very early that they have a strong-willed child. One-third can tell at birth. Two-thirds know by the youngster's first birthday, and 92 percent are certain by the third birthday. Parents of compliant children know it even earlier.

★ The temperaments of children tend to reflect those of their parents. Although there are many exceptions, two strong-willed parents are more likely to produce tough-minded kids and vice versa.

★ Parents of strong-willed children can expect a battle during the teen years, even if they have raised them properly. Fully 74 percent of strong-willed children rebel significantly during adolescence. The weaker the authority of the parents when the kids are young, the greater the conflict is in later years.

★ Incredibly, only 3 percent of compliant children experience severe rebellion in adolescence, and just 14 percent go into even mild rebellion.

★ The best news for parents of strong-willed children is the rapid decrease in their rebellion in young adulthood. It drops almost immediately in the early twenties and then trails off even more from there. Some are still angry into their twenties and early thirties, but by then the fire is gone for the majority. They peacefully rejoin the human community.

★ The compliant child is much more likely to be a good student than the strong-willed child. Nearly three times as many strong-willed children made Ds and Fs during the last two years of high school as did compliant children. Approximately 80 percent of compliant children were A and B students.

★ The compliant child typically enjoys higher self-esteem than the strong-willed child. It is difficult to overestimate the importance of this finding. Only 19 percent of compliant teenagers either disliked themselves (17 percent) or felt extreme self-hatred (2 percent). Of the very strong-willed teenagers, 35 percent disliked themselves and 8 percent experienced extreme self-hatred. The strong-willed child seems compelled from within to fuss, fight, test, question, resist, and challenge.

BEFORE YOU BEGIN

1. Which of these statistics did you find particularly surprising or interesting?

2. What personal examples have you seen that confirm the truth of Dr. Dobson's findings?

3. Which of your children are strong willed? How does this trait impact your relationship with them and with each other?

Laying It Out

One-size parenting advice doesn't fit all. Dr. Dobson expresses amazement that so many "experts" on parenting have failed to notice that some children are tougher to raise than others. He says that parents would never get that impression from reading the advice offered by an army of permissive psychologists, counselors, pediatricians, psychiatrists, and columnists for women's magazines. These so-called experts all seem convinced that rearing kids is as simple as falling off a log. For decades they have said that all a parent need do is give children lots of space, treat them like adults, and, if absolutely necessary, explain every now and then why they might want to consider behaving better. How nice it would be if that were true. But this rosy view is nonsense, according to Dobson.

POSITIVE PARENTING

A current example of permissive approaches to child rearing is referred to as "positive discipline," or the "positive parenting" movement. It sounds good, but it is little more than repackaged permissive claptrap. Consider the following advice Dr. Dobson found on the Oklahoma State Department of Health's "Positive Discipline" Web page. He observes:

> The advice reads, "The goal of discipline is not to control children and make them obey but to give them skills for making decisions, gradually gaining self-control, and being responsible for their own behavior." Instead of telling a child, "Don't hit the kitty" or "Stop kicking the table," they suggest that parents say, "Touch the kitty gently" or "Keep your feet on the floor." The Web site goes on to assert that, "Giving a child choices allows him some appropriate power over his life and encourages decision making." Parents are advised to "redirect" childish behavior. For example, if a child is throwing a truck around the house, instead of telling the child to stop, they suggest you say, "I can't let you throw your truck, but you may throw the ball outside." Or if the child is kicking a door, you are to explain,

"You may not kick the door, but you may kick this ball or plastic milk jug." Their suggestion for dealing with willful defiance is to ignore it or to allow the child to engage in "something pleasant" until he or she cools off.

Dr. Dobson calls this ridiculous advice. Note how hard the parent must work to avoid being the leader at home. What's wrong with explaining to a child exactly what you want him or her to do and expecting obedience in return? Why is it unacceptable for a parent to insist that a child who is engaging in destructive or irritating behavior immediately cease and desist? Why not tell the child, "Kitties have feelings just like you do. You will not hit the kitty"?

LEAD OR BE REPLACED AS LEADER

Dr. Dobson teaches that children whose parents have never taken charge firmly are being deprived of a proper understanding of their mom's or dad's authority. It also keeps children from comprehending other forms of authority they will encounter outside the safety of the family's permissive cocoon. Sooner or later, that boy or girl will bump into a teacher, a police officer, a Marine Corps drill sergeant, or an employer who has never heard of positive discipline and who will expect orders to be carried out as specified. The child who has only heard "suggestions" for alternative behavior through the years, which he or she may choose to accept or reject, will not be prepared for the real world.

Parental leadership has to make a showing. Boys and girls must be taught what is and is not acceptable behavior; the responsibility to establish those boundaries is an assignment given to moms and dads by the Creator of families. Parents can't always wait around for logical consequences to do a job they should be doing themselves.

Of course, logical consequences have a place in child rearing. But one logical consequence of misbehavior might be sitting the child's wiggly bottom on a chair with instructions to think about why he must never spit in Mommy's face or run down a busy street or drive nails in the furniture or try to flush baby sister down the toilet.

The positive parenting books don't admit that these misbehaviors and a thousand others do happen—regularly in some families. They won't acknowledge that some mothers and fathers go to bed at night with pounding, throbbing headaches, wondering how raising kids became such an exhausting and nerve-racking experience. Willfulness is built into the nature of some kids. It is simply part of their emotional and intellectual package brought with them into the world.

BLANK SLATE THEORY

The early authorities in the field of child development denied what their eyes told them. They thought they had a better idea, concluding that babies come into the world devoid of individuality. Children, they said, are blank slates upon which the environment and experience will be written. John Locke and Jean-Jacques Rousseau, among others, promoted this notion and thereby confused the scientific understanding of children for decades. Most of the best-known psychologists in the world subscribed to this theory at one time or another, and many are still influenced by it.

The more accurate view, based on careful research, recognizes that while experience is very important in shaping the human personality, the "blank slate" hypothesis is a myth. Children don't start life at the same place. They bring with them an individuality that is uniquely their own, different from that of every other individual who has ever lived. Dr. Dobson calls this "the strength of the will." It varies greatly from child to child. He adds that if you have regular contact with children, you will be able to see this aspect of temperament, more or less, in living color.

HEREDITY

Heredity plays a much larger role in the development of human temperament than was previously understood. This is the conclusion of meticulous research conducted over many years at institutions like the University of Minnesota. The researchers there identified more than one hundred sets of identical twins that had been separated near the time of birth. The twins were raised in varying cultures, religions, and locations. They did not know each other until they were grown. Because each set of twins shared the same DNA, or genetic material, and therefore the same architectural design, the researchers could examine the impact of inheritance by comparing their similarities and differences on many variables. From these and other studies, it became clear that much of the personality, perhaps 70 percent or more, is inherited. Our genes influence such qualities as creativity, wisdom, loving-kindness, vigor, longevity, intelligence, and even the joy of living.

THE HUMANIST APPROACH TO CHILD REARING

Dr. Dobson explains that people who believe in innate goodness would have us believe that human beings are naturally unselfish, honest, respectful, kind to others, self-controlled, obedient to authority, etc. They think that children subsequently learn to do wrong when they are exposed to a corrupt and misguided society. Bad *experiences* are responsible for bad behavior, according to these folks. To raise healthy kids, then, it is the task of parents to provide a loving environment and then stay out of the way. Natural goodness will flow from within. It doesn't work that way, Dobson says.

This is the humanistic perspective on a child's nature. Most psychologists have accepted and taught this notion throughout the twentieth century, and millions of people believe it to be true. Only one thing is wrong with the concept. It is entirely inaccurate.

Not only have nations warred against each other since the beginning of time, we also find among individuals a depressing incidence of murder, drug abuse, child molestation, prostitution, adultery, homosexuality, and dishonesty. How would we account for this pervasive evil in a world of people who are naturally inclined toward good? Have they really drifted into these antisocial and immoral behaviors despite their inborn tendencies? If so, surely *one* society could have preserved children's innate goodness. Where is it? Does such a place exist? No; although admittedly some societies are more moral than others. Still, none reflect the harmony that might be expected from the natural goodness theorists. Why not? Because their basic premise is wrong.

THINKING IT THROUGH

1. Share some examples of prodigal stories. Would you agree that strong-willed children are more likely to stray? Do you believe most will come back to the fold? Why or why not?

_____

_____

_____

_____

2. Explain what Dr. Dobson means by "logical consequences." What should or shouldn't parents do to short-circuit natural consequences of actions?

_____

_____

_____

_____

3. Do you agree that we are born sinful? Why or why not?

_____

_____

_____

_____

4. What traits/likes/dislikes have been impacted by heredity in your family?

_____

_____

_____

_____

5. Why has the positive parenting approach been so unsuccessful?

_____

_____

_____

_____

CASE STUDY:
There Is Hope

Dr. Dobson provides encouragement through the story of David Hernandez:

David and his parents came to the United States illegally from Mexico more than fifty years ago and nearly starved to death before they found work. They eventually survived by helping to harvest the potato crop throughout the state of California. During this era, David lived under trees or in the open fields. His father made a stove out of an oil drum half-filled with dirt. The open campfire was the centerpiece of their home.

David never had a roof over his head until his family finally moved into an abandoned chicken coop. His mother covered the boarded walls with cheap wallpaper, and David thought they were living in luxury. Then the city of San Jose condemned the area, and David's "house" was torn down. He couldn't understand why the community would destroy so fine a place.

Given this beginning, how can we explain the man that David Hernandez became? He graduated near the top of his class in high school and was granted a scholarship to college. Again, he earned high marks and four years later entered Loma Linda University School of Medicine. Once more, he scored in the top 10 percent of his class and continued in a residency in obstetrics and gynecology. Eventually, he served as a professor of obstetrics and gynecology at both Loma Linda University and the University of Southern California medical schools.

Dr. Dobson sums up his observations with these words: "God chooses to use individuals in unique ways. Beyond that mysterious relationship, we must simply conclude that some kids seem born to make it and others are determined to fail. Someone reminded me recently that the same boiling water that softens the carrot also hardens the egg. Likewise, some individuals react positively to certain circumstances and others negatively. We don't know why."

POINTS TO PONDER

1. How could such discipline and genius as David's come from these seemingly infertile circumstances?

_____

_____

_____

_____

2. Why have so many children of prominent and loving parents grown up in ideal circumstances only to reject it all for the streets?

_____

_____

_____

_____

3. Share some personal stories about men and women who beat the odds and found success and fulfillment.

_____

_____

_____

_____

DIGGING DEEPER

Scripture confirms that babies have temperaments or personalities before birth. In several references we learn that God knows and relates to unborn children as individuals. He said to the prophet Jeremiah, "Before I formed you in the womb I knew you, and before you were born I consecrated you; I appointed you a prophet to the nations" (Jeremiah 1:5, RSV).

The apostle Paul says we were also chosen before birth (see Ephesians 1:4). And in a remarkable account, we are told of the prenatal development of the twins Jacob and Esau. As predicted before their birth, one turned out to be rebellious and tough, while the other was something of a mama's boy. They were fighting before they were born and continued in conflict through much of their lives (see Genesis 25:22-27). Then later, in one of the most mysterious and disturbing statements in the Bible, the Lord said, "Jacob have I loved, but Esau have I hated" (Romans 9:13, KJV). Apparently, God discerned a rebellious nature in Esau before he was born and knew that he would not be receptive to the divine Spirit. God knew.

These examples tell us that unborn children are unique individuals with whom God is already acquainted. Dr. Dobson explains what the "owner's manual" has to say about human nature. Only the Creator of children can tell us how He made them, and He has done that in Scripture. It teaches that we are born in sin, having inherited a disobedient nature from Adam. King David said, "In sin did my mother *conceive* me" (Psalm 51:5, KJV, italics added), meaning that this tendency to do wrong was transmitted genetically. Paul said this sinful nature has infected every person who ever lived. "For *all* have sinned, and come short of the glory of God" (Romans 3:23, KJV, italics added). Therefore, with or without bad associations, children are naturally inclined toward rebellion, selfishness, dishonesty, aggression, exploitation, and greed. They don't have to be taught these behaviors. These behaviors are natural expressions of a child's humanness.

Bloody warfare has been the centerpiece of world history for more than five thousand years. People of every race and creed around the globe have tried to rape, plunder, burn, blast, and kill one another century after century. Peace has been but a momentary pause when they have stopped to reload! Plato said more than 2,350 years ago: "Only dead men have seen an end to war." He was right, and it will continue that way until the Prince of Peace comes.

Children, however, are not responsible for their sins until they reach an age of accountability—and that time frame is known only to God. On the other hand, parents should not be surprised when rebellious or mischievous behavior occurs. It *will* happen, probably by the eighteenth month or before. Anyone who has watched a toddler throw a temper tantrum when she doesn't get her way must be hard-pressed to explain how the phrase "innate goodness" became so popular! Did her mother or father model the tantrum for her, falling on the floor, slobbering, kicking, crying, and screaming? Probably not. Either way, the kid needs no demonstration. Rebellion comes naturally—although in some individuals it is more pronounced than in others.

For this reason, parents can and must train, mold, correct, guide, punish, reward, instruct, warn, teach, and love their kids during the formative years. Their purpose is to shape that inner nature and keep it from tyrannizing the entire family. Ultimately, however, only Jesus Christ can cleanse the heart and make it wholly acceptable to God. This is why Christian parents must point their children to the Savior.

1. Answer honestly: How do you feel about God treating Jacob and Esau differently, even from the womb? How do you make this fit with the idea of free will?

_____

_____

_____

_____

2. How do you respond to the idea that children are born as "blank slates"? What evidence have you seen to the contrary in your kids?

_____

_____

_____

_____

3. If sin is inevitable, why does God hold us accountable for our willfulness? After all, He made us that way.

_____

_____

_____

_____

4. Describe some positive and negative behaviors you think your child was born with. Also consider how appearance, attitudes, and aptitudes appear to be inborn.

_____

_____

_____

_____

TAKING IT HOME

Dr. Dobson concludes with two facts that must be understood. First, parents have been far too quick to take the credit or blame for the way their children turn out. Those with bright young superstars stick out their chests and say, "Look what we accomplished." Those with twisted and irresponsible kids wonder, _Where did we go wrong?_ Well, neither is entirely accurate. No one would deny that parents play an important role in the development and training of their children. But they are only part of the formula from which a young adult is assembled, as Dr. Dobson has explained.

Second, behavioral scientists have been far too simplistic in their explanation of human behavior. We are more than the aggregate of our experiences. We are more than the quality of our nutrition. We are more than our genetic heritage. We are more than our biochemistry. And we are more than our parents' influence. God has created us as unique individuals, capable of independent and rational thought that is not attributable to any other source. That is what makes the task of parenting so challenging and rewarding. Just when you think you have your kids figured out, you had better brace yourself! Something new is coming your way. Isn't that the truth?

So what are some practical hints for parenting young children? Remember this: They should only be disciplined for defiance, not for merely exploring their world. Many of the spankings given to toddlers can and should be avoided. Toddlers get in trouble most frequently because of their natural desire to touch, bite, taste, smell, and break everything within their grasp. This exploratory behavior is not aggressive; it is a valuable means for learning and should not be discouraged. Dr. Dobson has seen parents slap their two-year-olds throughout the day simply for investigating their world. This squelching of normal curiosity is not fair to the youngster, he reminds. It seems foolish to leave an expensive trinket where it will tempt the child and then scold him for taking the bait. If little fat fingers insist on handling the trinkets on the lower shelf, it is much wiser to distract the child with something else than to discipline him for his persistence. Toddlers cannot resist the offer of a new plaything. They are amazingly easy to interest in less fragile toys, and parents should keep a few alternatives available for use when needed. Dr. Dobson offers this as an easy answer to a difficult question.

A toddler should only be subjected to mild discipline when she openly defies her parents' spoken commands! If she runs the other way when called, purposely slams her milk glass onto the floor, dashes into the street while being told to stop, screams and throws a tantrum at bedtime, hits her friends—these forms of unacceptable behavior should be discouraged. Even in these situations, however, all-out spankings are not often required to eliminate the behavior. A parent's firm rap to the child's fingers or command to sit in a chair for a few minutes will convey the same message just as convincingly. Spankings should be reserved for a child's moments of greatest antagonism, usually occurring after the third birthday.

POINTS TO PONDER

1. Why is it that most children seem to have a need to take on those in authority over them?

_____

_____

_____

_____

2. What techniques have you found for effectively dealing with a young child's exploratory behavior?

_____

_____

_____

_____

3. What influences have come into play to make you the person and parent you are?

_____

_____

_____

_____

4. Share some examples of willful disobedience you've seen in your children or a friend's. What kind of discipline was most effective? least effective?

_____

_____

_____

_____

JOURNALING

1. Share some of your personal failings as a parent. Then write about the point where outside influences end and personal choices and responsibilities begin.

   _____

   _____

   _____

   _____

2. What is your greatest fear for your strong-willed child(ren)? What patterns of behavior or attitude do you see that could cause long-term pain and unhappiness? What can you do to help your child overcome these tendencies?

   _____

   _____

   _____

   _____

3. Look over the statistics at the beginning of this chapter. How can your child beat the numbers?

   _____

   _____

   _____

   _____

4. Confess a time when you disciplined a child inappropriately. Why did you respond as you did? What factors pushed you to respond out of harshness rather than love? Write out a prayer for greater discernment, wisdom, and grace.

_____

_____

_____

_____

5. How do you define the "all-out spankings" Dr. Dobson references? How often are they necessary? Write about the self-imposed limits you have set to ensure that your discipline never crosses the line to inappropriate punishment.

_____

_____

_____

_____

3

SHAPING THE WILL

Taken from chapter 4, "Shaping the Will"

GETTING IT STARTED

From a child's early years on, parents need to establish their position as the boss. Dr. Dobson writes, "When a real donnybrook occurs between generations, it is extremely important for parents to 'win.' Why? Because a child who behaves in ways that are disrespectful or harmful to himself or others often has a hidden motive. Whether he recognizes it or not, he is usually seeking to verify the existence and stability of the boundaries."

His point is that when parents remain confident and firm under fire, it creates a sense of security for the child. According to Dr. Dobson, parents must begin shaping the will of the particularly aggressive child very early in life. There is a difference, however, between crushing the will of a child and teaching the child to rein it in for his or her own good.

BEFORE YOU BEGIN

1. What is the difference between a child's "will" and a child's "spirit"?

_____

_____

_____

2. What does the idea of "shaping the will" mean to you?

_____

_____

_____

3. Did you ever feel that your spirit was crushed as a child? What effect did that have on you? How will you avoid doing the same thing to your children?

_____

_____

_____

4. Share some ideas of ways you can encourage your children to behave without resorting to corporal punishment.

_____

_____

_____

LAYING IT OUT

Let's review the six principles Dr. Dobson presents that help in shaping the will of a child.

1. Begin teaching respect for authority when children are very young.

It's never too early to begin instilling respect for authority within your children. This is the first step in helping children learn to control their powerful impulses. The most effective way to achieve that objective is keeping the tenor of the home pleasant, fun, and accepting, while demonstrating confident firmness. Once a child understands who is in charge, he or she can be held accountable for behaving in a respectful manner. The leadership of a parent plays a significant role in the child's development. By yielding to the loving authority (leadership) of his parents, a child learns to submit to other forms of authority that will confront him or her later in life.

Parents of assertive, independent children must establish their positions as strong but loving leaders when youngsters are in the preschool years. This is the first step toward helping them learn to control their powerful impulses. If the strong-willed child is allowed by indulgence to develop habits of defiance and disrespect during his or her early childhood, those characteristics will not only cause problems for the parents but also will ultimately handicap the child whose rampaging will was never brought under self-control.

Harshness, gruffness, and sternness are not effective in shaping a child's will. Likewise,

A pediatrician friend told me about a telephone call he received from the anxious mother of a six-month-old baby. "I think he has a fever," she said nervously. "Well," the doctor replied, "did you take his temperature?" "No," she said. "He won't let me insert the thermometer." There is trouble ahead for this shaky mother. There is even more danger for her son in the days ahead. He will quickly sense her insecurity and step into the power vacuum she has created. From there, it will be a wild ride all the way through adolescence.

constant whacking and threatening and criticizing are destructive and counterproductive. A parent who is mean and angry most of the time is creating resentment that will be stored and come roaring into the relationship during adolescence or beyond. Every opportunity should be taken, therefore, to strive for a balance of love and control in the home.

2. Define the boundaries before they are enforced.

This is an essential step before any disciplinary action can be taken. Children should know what is and what is not acceptable behavior before they are held responsible for it. It's not fair to hold children accountable for a rule that they never heard.

3. Distinguish between willful defiance and childish irresponsibility.

A child knocks over his milk because he's goofing around at the table or forgets to bring his bike in before it rains—those are examples of childish irresponsibility. And consequences follow. The milk must be cleaned up; the bike becomes rusty.

When accidents happen, patience and tolerance are the order of the day. If the foolishness was particularly pronounced for the age and maturity of the individual, Mom or Dad might want to have the youngster help with the cleanup or even work to pay for the loss. Otherwise, it's best to simply ignore these kinds of incidents.

Willful defiance of parental authority is far different, however. This occurs when a child shouts, "I will not!" or "You shut up!" or "You can't make me." These behaviors represent a willful, haughty spirit and a determination to disobey. These types of challenges to a parent's authority must be dealt with immediately. When mothers and fathers fail to be the boss in a moment like that, they create for themselves and their families a potential lifetime of heartache. Dr. Dobson believes a mild and appropriate spanking is the discipline of choice for a hot-tempered child between twenty months and ten years of age.

> "Some [misbehavior] should be overlooked and taken no notice of [referring to childish irresponsibility], and others mildly reproved. But no willful transgressions ought to ever be forgiven children without chastisement, more or less as the nature and circumstances of the offense shall require."
>
> —**Susanna Wesley,** *mother of nineteen*

4. Reassure and teach after the confrontation is over.

After a confrontation in which the parent has demonstrated his or her right to lead, most youngsters will probably need a time to be loved and reassured. Take this teachable moment to explain your love for the child and why you were disciplining the child. For Christian families, it is extremely important to pray with the child at this time, admitting to God that we all have sinned and that no one is perfect.

Nothing is more destructive to parental leadership than for a mother or father to equivocate during that struggle. When parents consistently lose those battles, resorting to tears and screaming and other signs of frustration, some dramatic changes take place in the way they are seen by their children.

5. Avoid impossible demands.

Be absolutely sure that your child is capable of delivering what you require. For example, never punish the child for wetting the bed involuntarily, not becoming potty trained by one year of age, or doing poorly in school when he or she is incapable of academic success. Be reasonable in what you're asking. To do otherwise puts undue pressure on a child to perform.

For example, most two-year-olds can no more fold their hands and sit quietly in church than they can swim the Atlantic Ocean. They squirm and churn and burn every second of their waking hours. No, this child should not be punished. He should be left in the nursery where he can shake the foundations without disturbing the worshippers.

6. Let love be your guide!

A relationship that is characterized by genuine love and affection is likely to be a healthy one, even though some parental mistakes and errors are inevitable.

THINKING IT THROUGH

1. How did you react to authority figures when you were young? How would you describe your child(ren)'s reaction to authority within the home? outside the home?

   _____

   _____

   _____

2. Think of the last nose-to-nose confrontation you had with one of your children. Who won? What do you think your child thought of you as a result of that confrontation and how it was resolved? What could you do differently if the confrontation were to take place today?

   _____

   _____

   _____

3. In what ways do you show your child(ren) that you are the boss? In what situations has it been difficult to establish your authority?

   _____

   _____

   _____

4. Think of your parenting style. Are you a drill sergeant, constantly giving orders, or a professional negotiator for your child's obedience? What would be a better style? What steps could you take to change your current pattern?

_____

_____

_____

_____

5. Recall an example of willful defiance from your child(ren). What about childish irresponsibility? How do you distinguish between the two?

_____

_____

_____

_____

6. Dobson writes: "When you have been challenged, it is time for you to take charge—to defend your right to lead. When mothers and fathers fail to be the boss in a moment like that, they create for themselves and their families a potential lifetime of heartache." How do you react to that statement? What have you experienced that either corroborates Dr. Dobson's statement or disagrees with it?

_____

_____

_____

_____

7. Let's step back a moment and look at "someone else's" problems. How would you maintain your cool and your authority if Junior began throwing a tantrum in the middle of the grocery store aisle or if Sissy refused to go to bed at the end of a long, hard day? Talk about tactics and techniques that have worked for you.

_____

_____

_____

CASE STUDY:
Dealing with Your Strong-Willed Child

Tim, my six-year-old, loves to use silly names whenever he speaks to my husband and me. For example, this week it's been "you big hot dog." Nearly every time he sees me now he says, "Hi, hot dog." Before that it was "dummy," then "moose" (after he studied *M* for moose in school). I know it's silly and it's not a huge problem, but it gets so annoying after such a long time. He's been doing this for a year now. How can we get him to talk to us with more respect, calling us Mom or Dad, instead of hot dog and moose?
—Leslie

Dr. Dobson responded to Leslie by first noting that the child has been using humor as a tactic of defiance. He suggested that it was time for Tim's parents to sit down and talk with him. They need to tell Tim that he is being disrespectful and that the next time he calls either parent a name of any kind, he will be punished.

Of course, explains Dobson, the parent must then be prepared to deliver on the promise, because Tim will continue to challenge until a spanking or other appropriate discipline takes the fun out of it. That's the way boys like Tim are made. If that response never comes, his insults will probably become more pronounced, ending in adolescent nightmares. Appeasement for a strong-willed child is an invitation to warfare.

POINTS TO PONDER

1. Would you classify Tim's behavior as childish irresponsibility or willful defiance, according to Dobson's definitions? Explain your answer. Why doesn't appeasement work?

2. How do you respond to Leslie's assessment that Tim's behavior is "not a huge problem"?

3. How would you handle Tim's behavior? What advice would you give Leslie?

4. When have you had a similar experience to Leslie's? What did you do?

_____

_____

_____

_____

5. Dr. Dobson describes some parents as being "spineless jellyfish who are unworthy of respect or allegiance." Have you seen an example of this type of parenting? What happens to the children of "jellyfish"? How do you plan to show loving leadership in your home?

_____

_____

_____

_____

Dr. Dobson tells another story of a mom confronting her tough-minded four-year-old daughter. The child was demanding her own way, and the mother was struggling to hold her own.

"Jenny," said the mother, "you are just going to have to do what I tell you to do. I am your boss. The Lord has given me the responsibility for leading you, and that's what I intend to do!"

Jenny thought that over for a minute and then asked, "How long does it have to be that way?"

Already at four years of age, this child was anticipating a day of freedom when no one could tell her what to do. Something deep within her spirit longed for control. Watch for

Never forget this fact: The classic strong-willed child craves power from the time he's a toddler and even earlier. Since Mom is the nearest adult who is holding the reins, he will hack away at her until she lets him drive his own buggy.

the same phenomenon in your child, Dobson warns. If he or she is a toughie, it will show up soon.

DIGGING DEEPER

The New Testament, which the Scripture tells us is "God-breathed" (2 Timothy 3:16), speaks eloquently to this point of loving leadership. We read in 1 Timothy 3:4-5, "He [speaking of the father] must have proper authority in his own household, and be able to control and command the respect of his children" (PHILLIPS). Colossians 3:20 expresses this divine principle to the younger generation: "Children, obey your parents in all things: for this is well pleasing unto the LORD" (KJV). No place in the Bible are little ones designated as co-discussants at a conference table, deciding what they will and will not accept from the older generation.

Why is parental authority so vigorously supported throughout the Bible? The leadership of parents plays a significant role in the development of a child, Dobson explains. By yielding to the loving authority (leadership) of her parents, a child learns to submit to other forms of authority that will confront her later in her life. Without respect for leadership, there is anarchy, chaos, and confusion for everyone concerned.

There is an even more important reason for the preservation of authority in the home. Children who are acquainted with it learn to yield to the benevolent leadership of God Himself. It is a fact that a child identifies his parents with God in the early days, whether the adults want that role or not. Specifically, most children see God the way they perceive their earthly fathers (and, to a lesser degree, their mothers).

We disappoint our children at times—when we're too tired to be what they need from us—times when our human frailties are all too apparent. Dr. Dobson has found that the older our offspring become, the greater the gap between who we are and who they thought we were—especially during the storms of adolescence. We may not want to represent God to our son and daughter, but that's how they think of us, whether we like it or not.

In short, the Creator has given parents the awesome responsibility of representing Him to their children. As such, they should reflect two aspects of divine nature to the next generation. First, our heavenly Father is a God of unlimited love, and our children must become acquainted with His mercy and tenderness through our own love toward them. But make no mistake about it: Our Lord is also the possessor of majestic authority! A sovereign God orders the universe, requires obedience from His children, and warns that "the wages of sin is death" (Romans 6:23). To show our little ones love without authority is as serious a distortion of God's nature as to reveal an iron-fisted authority without love.

From this perspective, then, a child who has "negotiated" with his parents and teachers only during times of intense conflict has probably not learned to submit to the authority of the Almighty. This is a problem. If this youngster is allowed to behave disrespectfully to Mom and Dad, sassing them and disobeying their specific orders, then it is most unlikely that he will turn his face up to God about twenty years later and say humbly, "Here am I, Lord; send me!" To repeat: a child learns to yield to the authority of God by first learning to submit to (rather than bargain with) the leadership of his parents.

The apostle Paul wrote to Timothy about a godly church leader, "He must be one who manages his own household well, keeping his children under control with all dignity" (1 Timothy 3:4, NASB). Why is it important for children to be "under control"? Was Paul giving parents the right to browbeat their children, disregard their feelings, and instill fear and anxiety in them? Of course not, Dr. Dobson replies. Paul teaches a wonderful balance in this letter and in Ephesians 6:4. This passage reads, "Fathers, do not exasperate your children; instead, bring them up in the training and instruction of the Lord."

1. Do you have control of your children? What does that mean, and how do you keep from exasperating your children?

_____

_____

_____

_____

2. Why is being in charge as a parent not simply forcing children to cater to the whims of oppressive, power-hungry adults, as some would have us believe? What are the spiritual reasons for strong parental leadership?

_____

_____

_____

_____

3. At what age should a child begin to have a voice and vote in family affairs? How do you help a child develop personal autonomy? Why is this so important?

_____

_____

_____

_____

4. Consider that kids often see their fathers as representations of God. What kind of pressure does that put on parents to correctly model love and grace and leadership?

_____

_____

_____

_____

TAKING IT HOME

The healthiest approach to child rearing is found in the safety of the middle ground between disciplinary extremes. This reasonable parenting style can be illustrated with this little diagram, taken from Dr. Dobson's first book, *Dare to Discipline*.

Children tend to thrive best in an environment where these two ingredients, love and control, are present in balanced proportions. When the scale tips in either direction, problems usually begin to develop at home. Unfortunately, parenting styles in a culture tend to sweep back and forth like a pendulum from one extreme to the other.

POINTS TO PONDER

1. Read 1 Timothy 3:4-5 and Ephesians 6:4 again. Describe how you currently keep a balance between controlling your children and not exasperating them.

_____

_____

_____

_____

2. How would you describe which side of the balance you lean toward right now? List at least two practical steps you can take to make this balance work better in your household.

_____

_____

_____

_____

3. Between now and the next lesson, look for examples of power struggles between children and parents. (These can come from your own experience or others you witness outside the home.) List them here.

_____

_____

_____

_____

4. Before the next lesson, identify at least one area of power struggle with your child that you currently face. Using the six principles we have just reviewed, design a strategy for winning that power struggle with your child.

_____

_____

_____

_____

5. If appropriate, write a note to your parents expressing your gratitude for all they did to keep you on track despite the difficulties involved.

_____

_____

_____

_____

JOURNALING

1. Ask God to bring to mind examples of His grace to you. Consider times that you have felt unworthy of His love and deserving of His discipline. Reflect on what these thoughts can teach you about your relationship with your children.

_____

_____

_____

_____

2. What do you consistently do that exasperates your children? Get to the root of the conflict and come up with some practical solutions to avoid future unnecessary conflict.

_____

_____

_____

_____

3. How are your strong-willed children most like you and your spouse? What tactics did your parents use to cope with your sometimes outrageous behavior?

_____

_____

_____

_____

4. Record some of your parenting victories from the week. When do things seem to go best? worst? Analyze the trigger points that set you off or put you over the edge.

_____

_____

_____

_____

5. Write down some of the continuing struggles you're facing. Pray for strength and hope.

_____

_____

_____

_____

4

PROTECTING THE SPIRIT

Taken from chapter 5, "Protecting the Spirit"

GETTING IT STARTED

Dr. Dobson points out that the human spirit is delicate. It reflects the self-concept or the sense of worthiness that a child feels. As the most fragile characteristic in human nature and one that is especially vulnerable to rejection, ridicule, and failure, it must be handled with great care.

How, then, are we to shape the will while preserving the spirit? This is accomplished, Dr. Dobson explains, by establishing reasonable boundaries in advance and then enforcing them with love, while avoiding any implications that a child is unwanted, unnecessary, foolish, ugly, dumb, burdensome, embarrassing, or regrettable. Any accusation or reckless comment that assaults the worth of a child, such as "You are so stupid!" can do lifelong damage. Dr. Dobson has seen the devastating results firsthand.

Other damaging remarks include "Why can't you make decent grades in school like your sister?" "You have been a pain in the neck ever since the day you were born!" "I told your mother it was stupid to have another child," "There are times when I would like to put you up for adoption," and "How could anyone love a fat slob like you?" Would parents actually say such hurtful things to a child? Unfortunately, Dr. Dobson says, they can and they do. We are all capable of hurling harsh words at a child or teenager when we are intensely angry or frustrated. Once such mean, cutting words have left our lips, even though we may repent a few hours later, they have a way of burning into a child's soul where they can remain alive and virulent for the next fifty years.

The circumstances that precipitate a hurtful comment for a child or teen are irrelevant to their impact. Dr. Dobson explains it this way: "Even though a child pushes you to the limit, frustrating and angering you to the point of exasperation, you will nevertheless pay a price for overreacting. Let's suppose you lose your poise and shout, 'I can't stand you! I wish you belonged to someone else.' Or 'I can't believe you failed another test. How could a son of mine be so stupid!' Even if every normal parent would also have been agitated in the same situation, your child will not focus on his misbehavior or failure in the future. He is likely to forget what he did to cause your outburst. But he will recall the day you said you didn't want him or that he was stupid. It isn't fair, but neither is life."

Dr. Dobson wants parents to be mindful that everything they say has lasting meaning for a child. The child may forgive you later for "setting the fire," but how much better it would have been to have stayed cool. You can learn to do that with prayer and practice.

BEFORE YOU BEGIN

1. Recall hurtful words spoken to you as a child. How did they make you feel then? And now?

_____

_____

_____

_____

2. What have you said to your son or daughter that you wish had remained unspoken? Explain the situation and how you wish you had handled it.

_____

_____

_____

_____

3. Under what circumstances are you most likely to fly off the handle and say unkind words to your child?

_____

_____

_____

_____

4. What's the best memory you have of encouraging words spoken to you by your parents? If you're having difficulty coming up with an example, discuss how this lack of positive words has impacted your adult relationship with them.

_____

_____

_____

_____

5. What can you do to bolster a child you know who rarely, if ever, gets positive reinforcement in the home?

_____

_____

_____

_____

LAYING IT OUT

SHAPING WITHOUT BREAKING

Our objective as parents, Dr. Dobson says, is not simply to shape the will but to do so without breaking the spirit. To understand this dual objective of parenting, we need to clarify the distinction between the will and the spirit. First, let's talk about the will, which represents one's deeply ingrained desire to have his or her way.

Dr. Dobson explains that the self-will of a very independent child may be fully operational at birth. It is remarkable how early the will can make its presence known. Studies of the neonatal period indicate that at two or three days of age, an infant is capable of manipulating parents to get what he or she wants and needs. A professor at the University of Chicago released a study concluding that long before the child can talk, he or she is able to size up adults and learn how to interact with them to his or her advantage. This finding would not be surprising to the parents of strong-willed infants who have walked the floor in the wee small hours, listening to their tiny baby making his or her wishes abundantly clear.

THE STRENGTH OF THE WILL

A year or two later, some toddlers can become so angry that they are capable of holding their breath until they lose consciousness. Anyone who has ever witnessed this full measure of rage has been shocked by its power. It can also be quite audacious. Dr. Dobson shared this story:

> The mother of one headstrong three-year-old told me her daughter refused to obey a direct command because, as she put it, "You're just a mommy, you know!" Another toddler screamed every time her mother grabbed her hand to guide her through a parking lot. She would yell at the top of her lungs: "Let go! You're hurting me!" The embarrassed mother, who was just trying to ensure her child's safety, would then have to deal with the hostile looks of other shoppers who thought she was abusing her child.

Willfulness is a fascinating component of the human personality. It is not fragile or wobbly. It can and must be molded, shaped, and brought under the authority of parental leadership. News stories often describe suicidal adults who stand on ledges or bridges, threatening to jump. Some of them have defied the combined forces of the Army, the Navy, and the Marine Corps, which sought desperately to save their lives. Even though these people had been emotionally sandbagged by life, their determination to control their own destiny remained intact and functional.

Parents will not harm a child by taking steps to gain control of a child's rebellious nature, Dr. Dobson says, even though such wresting of power sometimes involves confrontation, sternness, warnings, and, when appropriate, reasonable punishment. Only by accepting the inevitable challenges to parental authority and then by "winning" at those critical moments can parents teach a headstrong boy or girl civilized behavior. And only then will that child be given the ability to control his or her own impulses in the years to come.

Dr. Dobson made this topic a centerpiece of his book *Bringing Up Boys.* The following quote should be especially relevant for parents who are dealing with a sometimes irritating strong-willed child.

> [Words] are so easy to utter, often tumbling out without much reason or forethought. Those who hurl criticism or hostility at others may not even mean or believe what they have said. Their comments may reflect momentary jealousy, resentment, depression, fatigue, or revenge. Regardless of the intent, harsh words sting like killer bees. Almost all of us, including you and me, have lived through moments when a parent, a teacher, a friend, a colleague, a husband, or a wife said something that cut to the quick. That hurt is now sealed forever in the memory bank. That is an amazing property of the spoken word. Even though a person forgets most of his or her day-by-day experiences, a particularly painful comment may be remembered for decades. By contrast, the individual who did the damage may have no memory of the encounter a few days later. [Senator] Hillary Rodham Clinton told a story about her father, who never affirmed her as a child. When she was in high school, she brought home a straight-A report card. She showed it to her dad, hoping for a word of commendation. Instead, he said, "Well, you must be attending an

easy school." Thirty-five years later the remark still burns in Mrs. Clinton's mind. His thoughtless response may have represented nothing more than a casual quip, but it created a point of pain that has endured to this day.

THINKING IT THROUGH

1. Share some dramatic examples of tiny but strong-willed children. What family stories do you have about truly legendary strong-willed behavior?

_____

_____

_____

_____

2. When have you felt uncomfortable because your strong-willed child made a fuss in a public place? What happened, and how did you gain the upper hand in the conflict? If you didn't, what could you have done differently?

_____

_____

_____

_____

3. How do you define "civilized behavior" in children? What societal influences make it more difficult to teach kids these essentials? How can we counteract those forces?

_____

_____

_____

_____

4. How old was your child when you were able to determine you had a strong-willed soul on your hands? What were the signs?

_____

_____

_____

_____

CASE STUDY:
The Problem Child

Dear Dr. Dobson:

More than anything else in this world, I want to have a happy family. We have two girls, ages three and five, and a boy who is ten. They don't get along at all. The boy and his father don't get along either. And I find myself screaming at the kids and sitting on my son to keep him from hitting and kicking his sisters.

His teacher of the past year thought he needed to learn better ways of getting along with his classmates. He had some problems on the playground and had a horrible time on the school bus. And he didn't seem to be able to walk from the bus stop to our house without getting in a fight or throwing rocks at somebody. So I usually pick him up and bring him home myself.

He is very bright but writes poorly and hates to do it. He is impulsive and quick-tempered (we all are now). He is tall and strong. Our pediatrician says he has "everything going for him." But Jake seldom finds anything constructive to do. He likes to watch television, play in the water, and dig in the dirt.

We are very upset about his diet but haven't been able to do anything about it. He drinks milk and eats Jell-O and crackers and toast. In the past he ate lots of hot dogs and bologna, but not much lately. He also craves chocolate and bubble gum. We have a grandma nearby who sees that he gets lots of it. She also feeds him baby food. We haven't been able to do anything about that, either.

Jake's teachers, the neighbor children, and his sisters complain about his swearing and name-calling. This is really an unfortunate situation because we're always thinking of him in a bad light. But hardly a day goes by when something isn't upset or broken. He's been breaking windows since he was a toddler. One day in June he came home early from school and found the house locked, so he threw a rock through his bedroom window, broke it, and crawled in. Another day recently he tried the glass cutter on our bedroom mirror. He spends a great deal of time at the grandma's who caters to him. We feel she is a bad influence, but so are we when we're constantly upset and screaming.

Anyhow, we have what seems to be a hopeless situation. He is growing bigger and stronger but not any wiser. So what do we do or where do we go?

My husband says he refuses to take Jake anywhere ever again until he matures and "acts like a civilized human being." He has threatened to put him in a foster home. I couldn't send him to a foster home. He needs people who know what to do with him. Please help us if you can.

Mrs. T.

P.S. Our children are adopted and there isn't much of anything left in our marriage.

POINTS TO PONDER

1. What are the unique challenges that adoptive or foster parents face in raising strong-willed children? What responsibility do Jake's parents bear for the child he has become? How about Grandma's role? What is Jake's own share in the mess?

_____

_____

_____

_____

2. Do you think Jake's father actually meant what he said about putting him in a foster home? Why was that an inappropriate comment?

_____

_____

_____

_____

3. What would you say to encourage Jake's parents? What ideas would you share for helping Jake to do better in school?

_____

_____

_____

_____

4. How do you think Jake's sisters feel about him? What is behind Jake's maddening behavior?

_____

_____

_____

_____

5. What are some ideas to curb Jake from his use of foul language? How could his parents break him of this and other antisocial behaviors (rock throwing, fighting, etc.)?

_____

_____

_____

_____

DIGGING DEEPER

Words can hurt or heal. They are powerful.

If you doubt this, remember what John the disciple wrote. He said, "In the beginning was the Word, and the Word was with God, and the Word was God" (John 1:1). John was describing Jesus, the Son of God, who was identified personally with words. That makes the case about words as well as it will ever be demonstrated. Matthew, Mark, and Luke each record a related prophetic statement made by Jesus that confirms the eternal nature of His teachings. Jesus said, "Heaven and earth will pass away, but my words will never pass away" (Matthew 24:35). We remember what Jesus said to this hour, more than two thousand years later. Clearly, words matter.

The book of James contains additional wisdom about the impact of words:

> When we put bits into the mouths of horses to make them obey us, we can turn the whole animal. Or take ships as an example. Although they are so large and are driven by strong winds, they are steered by a very small rudder wherever the pilot wants to go. Likewise the tongue is a small part of the body, but it makes great boasts. Consider what a great forest is set on fire by a small spark. The tongue also is a fire, a world of evil among the parts of the body. It corrupts the whole person, sets the whole course of his life on fire, and is itself set on fire by hell. (James 3:3-6)

All parents have, at times, mistakenly allowed a cutting comment to fly out of their mouth. The dart sticks hard. If we tried for a hundred years, we couldn't take back a single remark, Dr. Dobson says.

He tells a story about the first year Shirley and he were married. She became angry with him about something that neither can recall today. In the frustration of the moment she said, "If this is marriage, I don't want any part of it." She didn't mean it and regretted her words almost immediately. An hour later they had reconciled and forgiven each other, but Shirley's statement could not be taken back. Through the years, Dr. and Mrs. Dobson have laughed about the incident. The point is, of course, that there is nothing either of them can do to erase the utterance of the moment.

Words are not only remembered for a lifetime, but if not forgiven, they endure beyond the chilly waters of death. We read in Matthew 12:36: "I tell you that men will have to give account on the day of judgment for every careless word they have spoken." Thank God, those of us who have a personal relationship with Jesus Christ are promised that our sins—and our harsh words—will be remembered against us no more and will be removed "as far as the east is from the west" (Psalm 103:12). Apart from that atonement, however, our words will follow us forever.

If we lose control and say something that deeply wounds a child, we should begin to repair the damage as quickly as possible—as in the game of golf. Dr. Dobson has many fanatic golfing friends who have tried in vain to teach him their game. They never give up even though, according to him, it is a lost cause. One of them told Dr. Dobson that he should immediately replace the divot after digging a hole in the green. He said that the quicker Dr. Dobson got that tuft of grass back in place, the faster its roots would reconnect.

Though his friend was talking about golf, Dr. Dobson was thinking about people. When you have hurt someone, whether a child, a spouse, or a colleague, you must dress the wound before infection sets in. Apologize, if appropriate. Talk it out. Seek to reconcile. The longer the "divot" bakes in the sun, the smaller its chances for recovery will be. Almost two thousand years ago, the apostle Paul wrote: "Do not let the sun go down while you are still angry" (Ephesians 4:26). That Scripture has often been applied to husbands and wives, but Dr. Dobson thinks it is just as valid with children.

A comment that means little to us at the time may stick and be repeated long after we are dead and gone, Dr. Dobson warns. By contrast, the warm and affirming things we say about our sons and daughters may be a source of satisfaction for decades. Again, it is all in the power of words.

POINTS TO PONDER

1. When have you set yourself on fire with sparks spraying from your tongue? When did you set a child's spirit on fire with anger? What pushed you over the edge, and how could you have better handled the encounter?

   _____

   _____

   _____

   _____

2. What is the difference between forgiveness and reconciliation? Can you have one without the other? Must one precede the other? Why?

   _____

   _____

   _____

   _____

3. What are some encouraging words that have stuck with you? Why do positive comments make such an impact?

_____

_____

_____

_____

4. Under what circumstances are you most likely to fly off the handle or run at the mouth? How can your spouse or a close friend help prevent you from saying things you'll later regret?

_____

_____

_____

_____

TAKING IT HOME

THE TROUBLE WITH JAKE

Let's return to Jake and consider what could be done to improve a situation that could spell enormous problems for the future of that family. What a sad plea for help. The writer was undoubtedly sincere when she wrote, "more than anything else in this world, I want to have a happy family." From the tone of her letter, however, it was unlikely that she ever realized that greatest longing. In fact, that specific need for peaceful coexistence and harmony apparently led to many of her problems with Jake. She lacked the courage to do battle with him. In short, Jake's parents made two very serious mistakes.

First, Mr. and Mrs. T. failed to shape Jake's will, although he was begging for their intervention. It is an unsettling thing to be your own boss at ten years of age—unable to find even *one* adult who is strong enough to earn your respect. Why else would Jake have broken every rule and attacked every symbol of authority? He waged war on his teacher at school, but she was also baffled by his challenge. All she knew to do was call his trembling mother and report that Jake needs to learn better ways of getting along with his classmates.

Mrs. T. and her husband were totally perplexed and frustrated. She responded by "screaming at the kids" and "sitting on [her] son" when he misbehaved. No one knew what to do with him. Even Grandma was a bad influence. Mom resorted to anger and high-pitched weeping and wailing. There is *no* more ineffective approach to child management than volcanic displays of anger.

TAKING CONTROL

Mrs. T. and her husband had totally abdicated their responsibility to provide leadership for their family. Note how many times she said, in essence, *we are powerless to act*. These parents were distressed over Jake's poor diet but wrote that they "haven't been able to do anything about it." Jake's grandmother fed him junk food and bubble gum, but they weren't able to do anything about that either. Likewise, they couldn't stop him from swearing or tormenting his sisters or breaking windows or throwing rocks at his peers. Why? Jake, not his parents, was in charge.

The T. family's second mistake was to assault Jake's wounded spirit with every conflict. Not only did they scream and cry and wring their hands in despair, but they also demeaned his sense of personal worth and dignity. His father shouted at him and demanded that he act like a civilized human being, or he'd never take his son anywhere again. On top of that, he even threatened to throw him out of the family and put him into a foster home.

With each accusation, Jake's self-esteem moved down another notch. But did these personal assaults make him sweeter and more cooperative? Of course not! He just became meaner, more bitter, and more convinced of his own worthlessness. You see, Jake's spirit had been crushed, but his will still raged at hurricane velocity. And sadly, he then turned his self-hatred on his peers and family.

How would Dr. Dobson have approached this defiant youngster? Here's the message he would have shared with Jake if he could have had Jake in his home for a period of time:

Jake, there are several things I want to talk over with you. First, you'll soon learn how much we love you in this house. I'm glad you're here, and I hope these will be the happiest days of your life. And you should know that I care about your feelings and problems and concerns. We invited you here because we wanted you to come, and you will receive the same love and respect that is given to our own children. If you have something on your mind, you can come right out and say it. I won't get angry or make you regret expressing yourself. Neither my wife nor I will ever intentionally do anything to hurt you or treat you unkindly. You'll see that these are not just empty promises that you're hearing. This is the way people act when they care about each other, and we already care about you.

But, Jake, there are some other things you need to understand. There are going to be some definite rules and acceptable ways of behaving in this home, and you are going to have to live within them, just as our other children do. I will have them written for you by tomorrow morning. You will carry your share of responsibilities and jobs, and your schoolwork will be given high priority each evening. And you need to understand, Jake, that my most important job as your guardian is to see that you behave in ways that are healthy to yourself and others. It may take you a week or two to adjust to this new situation, but you're going to make it and I'm going to be here to see that you do. And when you refuse to obey, I will punish you immediately. In fact, I'm going to be right on your neck until you figure out that you can't beat the system. I have many ways to make you miserable, and I'm prepared to use them when necessary. This will help you change some of the destructive ways you've been acting in recent years. But even when I must discipline you, know that I will love you as much as I do right now. Nothing will change that.

The first time Jake disobeyed what he knew to be definite instructions, Dr. Dobson would have reacted decisively. There would have been no screaming or derogatory accusations, although he would quickly discover that Dr. Dobson meant what he said. The following morning the two would have discussed the issue rationally, and Jake would be reassured of the family's love. The slate would be wiped clean and everyone would start over again.

POINTS TO PONDER

1. How do your children know when you're stressed or tired? How do you signal to them, "Watch out: I'm in a bad mood"?

2. When was the last time you apologized to your child? What kind of response did you get from him or her? What makes apologies so difficult? What are your children learning from your example?

3. How many chances should you give a child? When is immediate judgment required?

4. Why is keeping a child busy ineffective in preventing all behavioral problems? Give examples from your personal experience.

_____

_____

_____

_____

5. Is having a "happy family" a worthy goal? What do you think Jake's mom meant by that? What else do you hope for your children besides mere happiness?

_____

_____

_____

_____

JOURNALING

1. For what do you want to be remembered when you leave this world?

_____

_____

_____

_____

2. If you could take back words you've spoken, what would they be? What has happened in that relationship as a result of your words?

_____

_____

_____

_____

3. Write down your innermost thoughts about your own willfulness. How do you want God to shape and mold *you?*

_____

_____

_____

_____

4. Write some encouraging words for your spouse and children. Be sure you share those thoughts either in person or on a card.

_____

_____

_____

_____

5. If appropriate, confess your tendency to see the sour side of life, and write out a prayer to your heavenly Father that you would begin to use life-giving words in your communications with family and friends.

_____

_____

_____

_____

5

THE MOST COMMON MISTAKE

GETTING IT STARTED

Dr. Dobson has emphatically stated that trying to control children by displays of anger and verbal outbursts is the most ineffective approach to management. It not only doesn't work, he says, but it actually makes matters worse. Researchers at the University of Washington found that parents who attempt to control their children by yelling and insulting them are likely to cause even more disruptive and defiant behavior. Dr. Dobson explains it this way: "If you yell at your kids, they will yell back at you—and more! Furthermore, there is an interactive effect. As the child becomes more rebellious, the parent becomes even angrier."

When frustrated, most adults fall into that pattern of parenting. Educators often make the same mistake. Dr. Dobson once heard a teacher say on national television, "I like being a professional educator, but I hate the daily task of teaching. My children are so unruly that I have to stay mad at them all the time just to control the classroom." Dr. Dobson adds, "How utterly demoralizing to be required to be mean and bad-tempered day in and day out to keep kids from going wild. Yet many teachers (and parents) know of no other way to make them obey. Believe me, it is exhausting and counterproductive!"

He continues, "Consider your *own* motivational system. Suppose you are driving home from work one afternoon, exceeding the speed limit by forty miles per hour. A police officer stands on the corner, but there isn't much he can do in response to your driving. He has no car, no motorcycle, no badge, no gun, and no authority to write tickets. All he can do is scream insults at you and shake his fist as you pass. Would that cause you to slow down? Of course not! You might smile and wave as you hurry by. The officer's anger only emphasizes his impotence." You see the point. Angry parents are just as ineffective.

BEFORE YOU BEGIN

1. When have you seen the pattern Dr. Dobson describes: angry parents angering their children, who further anger their parents? How can the cycle be broken?

_____

_____

_____

2. What motivates you to do the right thing at work or in the home? What keeps your children in check? How can you guide them toward obedience?

_____

_____

_____

3. Does anger ever work? Can anger toward a child ever be justified? Explain.

_____

_____

_____

4. How much of your daily fatigue is caused by conflicts with your children, spouse, or others? What can you do to avoid such altercations?

_____

_____

_____

_____

5. Isn't some confrontation both necessary and healthy? Explain.

_____

_____

_____

_____

LAYING IT OUT

AGREE TO AGREE

Parents must present a united front, Dr. Dobson says, especially when children are watching. An issue on which you disagree can be discussed later in private. Unless both parents can come to a consensus, their children will begin to perceive that standards of right and wrong are arbitrary. They will also make end runs around the tougher parent to get the answer they want from the soft touch.

Here's the point of danger: Some of the most hostile, aggressive teenagers Dr. Dobson has ever seen come from family constellations where the parents have leaned in opposite directions in their discipline. Suppose the father is unloving and disinterested in the welfare of his kids. His approach is harsh and physical. He comes home tired and may knock them around if they get in his way. The mother is permissive by nature. She worries every day about the lack of love in the father-child relationships. Eventually she sets out to compensate for it. When Dad sends their son to bed without his dinner, Mom slips him milk and cookies. When Dad says no to a particular request, Mom finds a way to say yes. She lets the kids get away with murder because it is not in her spirit to confront them.

Dr. Dobson explains that under these circumstances, the authority figures in the family contradict each other and cancel each other out. Consequently, the child is caught in the middle and often grows up hating both parents. It doesn't always work that way, but the probability for trouble is high. The middle ground between extremes of love and control must be sought if we are to produce healthy, responsible children.

HERE COMES THE JUDGE

To help convey the importance of having authority over your children, Dr. Dobson has woven the following scenario:

> Imagine yourself tearing through a school zone one morning on the way to the office. You suddenly look in the rearview mirror and see a black-and-white squad car bearing down on you from behind. Eight red lights are flashing and the siren is screaming. The officer uses his loudspeaker to tell you to pull over to the curb. When you have stopped, he opens his door and approaches your window. He is six foot nine, has a voice like the Lone Ranger's, and wears a big gun on his hip. His badge is gleaming in the light. He is carrying a little leather-bound book of citations that you have seen before—last month. The officer speaks politely but firmly, "Sir, I have you on radar traveling sixty-five miles per hour in a twenty-mile-per-hour zone. May I see your driver's license, please?" The officer doesn't scream, cry, or criticize you. He doesn't have to. You become putty behind the wheel. You fumble nervously to locate the small plastic card in your wallet (the one with the picture you hate). Your hands get sweaty and your mouth is dry as a bone. Your heart pounds like crazy in your throat. Why are you so breathless? It is because the course of *action* that the police officer is about to take is notoriously unpleasant. It will dramatically affect your future driving habits or, if you do not change, even cause you to do a lot of walking in the days ahead.

Six weeks later you go before a judge to learn your fate. He is wearing a black robe and sits high above the courtroom. Again, you are a nervous wreck. Not because the judge yells at you or calls you names—but because he has the power to make your day a little more unpleasant.

Dr. Dobson believes that a parent's anger alone does not influence behavior unless it implies that something irritating is about to happen. By contrast, *disciplinary action* does cause behavior to change. Not only does anger not work, Dr. Dobson is convinced that it produces a destructive kind of disrespect in the minds of our children. They perceive that our frustration is caused by our inability to control the situation. We represent justice to them, yet we're on the verge of tears as we flail the air with our hands and shout empty threats and warnings.

Let's be clear. Dr. Dobson is not recommending that parents and teachers conceal their legitimate emotions from their children. Nor is he suggesting that we be like bland and unresponsive robots that hold everything inside. At times, when our boys and girls become insulting or disobedient to us, revealing our displeasure is entirely appropriate. In fact, it *should* be expressed at a time like that; otherwise, we will appear phony and wimpy. But expressing displeasure should never become a *tool* to get children to behave when we have run out of options and ideas. It is ineffective and can be damaging to the relationship between generations.

PUSHING THE LIMITS

Another interesting fact about children is that, having identified the circumstances immediately preceding disciplinary action, they will take their parents directly to that barrier and bump it repeatedly but will seldom go beyond it deliberately. Once or twice a child will ignore his or her mother's emotional fireworks, just to see if she has the courage to deliver on her promise. When that question has been answered, the child will do what she demands in the nick of time to avoid punishment.

Dr. Dobson has said that parental anger often signals to a child that the parents have reached their action line. Therefore, children obey, albeit reluctantly, only when Mom and Dad get mad, indicating that they will now resort to punishment. Often parents observe that the child's surrender occurs simultaneously with their anger, and they inaccurately conclude that their emotional explosion is what forced the youngster to yield. Thus, their anger seems necessary for control in the future. They have grossly misunderstood the situation. It's not the anger that triggers compliance; it's the child's belief that the parents are finally going to put their money where their mouth is.

Most parents (even those who are very permissive) have a point on the scale beyond which they will not be pushed. Dr. Dobson explains that inevitable punishment looms immediately across that line. Amazingly, children know precisely where their parents typically draw the line. We adults reveal our particular points of action to them in at least six or eight subtle ways. For example, only at those moments do we use their middle names ("Jessica Emily Smith, get in that tub!"); our speech becomes more staccato and abrupt ("Young! Lady! I! Told! You! . . . "); our faces turn red (an important clue); we jump from our chair; and the child knows it is time to cooperate. It's all a game.

Dr. Dobson has one message for every parent: You don't need *anger* to control children. You *do* need strategic action. If you don't take a stand with your child early, she is compelled by her nature to push you further. Terrible battles are inevitable, especially during the adolescent years. The hesitant and guilt-ridden parent who is most anxious to avoid confrontation often finds himself or herself screaming and threatening throughout the day and ultimately thrashing the child. Indeed, physical abuse may be the end result. However, if Mom and Dad have the courage and conviction to provide firm leadership from the earliest days of childhood, administering it in a context of genuine love, both generations will enjoy an atmosphere of harmony and respect.

THINKING IT THROUGH

1. What convinced you that anger is an ineffective tool?

_____

_____

_____

_____

2. When is it appropriate to let your children see your emotions? When should you hide your feelings from them?

_____

_____

_____

_____

3. In your mind, what is the worst offense a child can be guilty of (for example, disrespect, fighting, lying)? How do you respond when your child hits the buttons that set you off?

_____

_____

_____

_____

4. Why should parents agree on how to handle problems when they arise? Is compromise on discipline ever a good idea? Explain.

_____

_____

_____

_____

CASE STUDY:
The Trouble with Henry

Henry is in the second grade and a constant whirlwind of activity. He has been wiggling and giggling since he got up that morning, but incredibly, he still has excess energy that needs to be burned. His mom is not in the same condition. She has been on her feet since staggering out of bed at 5:30 A.M. She fixed breakfast for the family, cleaned up the mess, got Dad off to work, sent Henry to school, and if she is employed, dropped off the younger kids at a day care center and rushed off to work. Or if she is a stay-at-home mom, she settled into a long day of trying to keep the preschoolers from killing each other. By late afternoon, she has put in nine hours of work without a rest. . . .

Henry arrives home from school in a decidedly mischievous mood. He can't find anything interesting to do, so he begins to irritate his uptight mother. He teases his little sister to the point of tears, pulls the cat's tail, and spills the dog's water. Mom is nagging by this time, but Henry acts like he doesn't notice. Then he goes to the toy closet and begins tossing out games and boxes of plastic toys and dumping out enough building blocks to construct a small city. Mom knows that someone is going to have to clean up all that mess, and she has a vague notion about who will get that assignment. The intensity of her voice is rising again. She orders him to the bathroom to wash his hands in preparation for dinner. Henry is gone for fifteen minutes. When he returns, his hands are still dirty. Mom's pulse is pounding through her arteries by this time and there is a definite migraine sensation above her left eye. . . .

Finally, Henry's bedtime arrives. But he does not *want* to go to bed, and he knows it will take his harassed mother at least thirty minutes to get him there. Henry does not do *anything* against his wishes unless his mother becomes very angry and blows up at him. Henry is sitting on the floor, playing with his games. Mom looks at her watch and says, "Henry, it's nearly eight o'clock [a thirty-minute exaggeration], so gather up your toys and go take your bath." Now Henry and Mom both know that she didn't mean for him to immediately take a bath. She merely wanted him to start thinking about taking his bath. She would have fainted dead away if he had responded to her empty command.

Approximately ten minutes later, Mom speaks again. "Now, Henry, it's getting later and you have school tomorrow; I want those toys picked up and then I want you in that tub!" She still does not expect Henry to obey, and he knows it. Her real message is, "We're getting closer, Hank." Henry shuffles around and stacks a box or two to demonstrate that he heard her. Then he settles down for a few more minutes of play. Six minutes pass and Mom issues another command, this time with more passion and threat in her voice, "Now listen, young man, I told you to get a move on, and I meant it!" To Henry, this means he must get his toys picked up and m-e-a-n-d-e-r toward the bathroom door. If his mother rapidly pursues him, then he must carry out the assignment posthaste. However, if Mom's mind wanders before she performs the last step of this ritual, or if the phone miraculously rings, Henry is free to enjoy a few minutes' reprieve.

What's a mother to do?

POINTS TO PONDER

1. How often have you seen a troublesome "Henry" in the mall or grocery store? What are some of the weak, worthless approaches you've seen parents take to try to deal with the problem?

_____

_____

_____

_____

2. Share a list of your daily stresses and expand on the reasons you find it nearly impossible to get everything done. What would make life easier for you?

_____

_____

_____

_____

3. Provide some ideas of your perfect getaway. Note the similarities and differences between what you and your spouse do to relax.

_____

_____

_____

_____

4. Can you reason a child into obedience? Why or why not?

_____

_____

_____

_____

5. How does your child know when he or she has pushed you beyond the limit?

_____

_____

_____

_____

DIGGING DEEPER

A SCRIPTURAL PERSPECTIVE ON ANGER

Many view God as a wrathful being who waits in the wings to lower the boom. We see Him as an angry God of judgment. Some envision God according to the description in Isaiah 30:30: "The LORD will cause men to hear his majestic voice and will make them see his arm coming down with raging anger and consuming fire, with cloudburst, thunderstorm and hail." While it is true that our God is all-powerful and will judge the world someday, that isn't the whole picture of who He is. Sadly, our earthly father may have bolstered this view of a wrathful God if he frequently resorted to anger over reason.

Or consider Isaiah 54:8: "'In a surge of anger I hid my face from you for a moment, but with everlasting kindness I will have compassion on you,' says the LORD your Redeemer." We, too, need to take a break at times to hide our faces and collect ourselves. This allows us to let the anger drain out so that we don't respond with the rage that so often blocks both ears and brain.

Thankfully, however, Psalm 30:5 reminds us, "His anger lasts only a moment, but his favor lasts a lifetime; weeping may remain for a night, but rejoicing comes in the morning." And Psalm 86:15 proclaims, "But you, O Lord, are a compassionate and gracious God, slow to anger, abounding in love and faithfulness."

Job 18:4 speaks about rage: "You who tear yourself to pieces in your anger, is the earth to be abandoned for your sake? Or must the rocks be moved from their place?" How often do we shake the house, tearing ourselves and our children to pieces in the process because of our uncontrolled anger?

When we're angry, we often sin because we're not thinking clearly. Reflect on the story of the ungrateful servant from Matthew 18:34: "In anger his master turned him over to the jailers to be tortured, until he should pay back all he owed." How foolish. The servant's thoughtless greed and rage caused him to make a mistake that would cost him his own freedom.

God's Word has some clear directives about how we should respond when upset. Proverbs 15:1 says, "A gentle answer turns away wrath, but a harsh word stirs up anger." Contrast the picture of the wise man with the fool who "gives full vent to his anger" (Proverbs 29:11). Another colorful verse states it this way: "For as churning the milk produces butter, and as twisting the nose produces blood, so stirring up anger produces strife" (Proverbs 30:33).

Anger is not the answer. For truly "man's anger does not bring about the righteous life that God desires" (James 1:20). We can decide whether we'll respond to our children with compassion or outrage. And that's one choice we should make *before* conflict arises.

POINTS TO PONDER

1. How do you see God, relative to anger? How much of this image is based on your perception of and relationship with your earthly father?

2. What strategies have you found successful in defusing your own anger?

3. Share some examples of poor decisions you've made when under the influence of rage.

4. How do harsh words stir up wrath?

_____

_____

_____

_____

TAKING IT HOME

Remember little Henry, the delinquent in training? Whenever Mom wants Henry to do something he dislikes, she progresses through graduated steps of phony anger, beginning with calmness and ending with a red flush and threats. Henry does not have to move until she reaches her flash point, which signals that she is ready to do something about it. How foolish this game is. Since Mom controls Henry with empty threats, she must stay half-irritated all the time. Her relationship with her children is contaminated, and she ends each day with a pulsing headache. She can never count on instant obedience because she takes at least twenty or thirty minutes to work up a believable degree of anger.

By her ultimate display of anger at bedtime, Mom makes it clear to Henry that she is through warning and is now ready to take definite action. Only when she blows up does he get in the tub, leading her to believe that her anger has produced his obedience. She is wrong! It was not her anger that sent Henry to the tub—it was the *action* he believed to be imminent. Her anger was nothing more than a tip-off that Mom was frustrated enough to spank his bottom. Henry *cares* about that!

In the absence of action early in the conflict, the parent usually ends up punishing anyway. The consequences are also more likely to be severe because by then the adult is irritated and may be out of control. And instead of administering the discipline in a calm and judicious manner, the parent has become unnerved and frustrated, swinging wildly at the belligerent child.

Dr. Dobson suggests a different approach. Henry's mother should forewarn him that he has fifteen more minutes, so he knows that playtime is coming to an end. At that point setting a timer in the kitchen would be a good idea. When the fifteen minutes passes, Mom should quietly tell Henry to go take his bath. If he doesn't move immediately, she could take Henry's face in her hands, look him straight in the eye, and say with conviction but not with frustration, "Do it *now*. Do you understand?" If the lad believes in his heart of hearts that his mother is prepared to punish him for delaying, no punishment will be necessary. If Henry learns that this procedure or some other unpleasantness is invariably visited upon him in such a moment, he will move before the consequences ensue.

Then the child will have a choice to make, and he will know the advantages to him of obeying his mother's wishes. She need not scream. She need not threaten to shorten his life. She need not become upset. She is in command. Of course, Mother will have to prove two or three times that she will apply the pain or other punishment if necessary. Occasionally throughout the coming months, Henry will check to see if she is still at the helm. That question is easily answered.

POINTS TO PONDER

1. Why do some moms say that dads have it easier? Is that fair? Why or why not?

2. What does it mean to discipline with love? Why does discipline help a child learn to govern his or her actions?

3. What realistic boundaries have you set with your children when it comes to bedtime rituals? How successful have they been?

_____

_____

_____

4. Why does it seem that some parents have no problem controlling their children and others are worn ragged by the task? What's the difference in approach that you've noted in yourself and others?

_____

_____

_____

5. What practical ways have you learned to place responsibility on your child for getting to school on time, keeping clothes clean for school, and doing schoolwork? Give some creative examples of how you've avoided stress by setting reasonable, loving boundaries.

_____

_____

_____

JOURNALING

1. List some surefire points of conflict looming before you (first day of school, a new driver in the family, job change, etc.), and write down how these issues unnerve, upset, or worry you. Talk over your concerns with your heavenly Father.

_____

_____

_____

_____

2. Think back to the days before children. List ways that life is now very different. Beware that you don't cast your thoughts in terms of negative or positive differences. Now share what you've learned about the nature of God through your children.

_____

_____

_____

_____

3. Consider ways you could turn over greater responsibility to your children. Are you helping to move them toward independence or exhibiting unhealthy patterns of control?

4. Ask God to show you ways you've harmed your child's spirit. Openly journal about times you've felt your own spirit crushed by your spouse, children, friends, or family. Pray about how you can address these issues and avoid future hurt and pain.

6

DISCIPLINE & CORPORAL PUNISHMENT

Taken from chapter 7, "Gearing Discipline to the Needs of Children," and chapter 8, "Corporal Punishment & the Strong-Willed Child"

GETTING IT STARTED

Dr. Dobson would be the first person to acknowledge that corporal punishment can be harmful when used wrongly. It is possible—even easy—to create an aggressive child who has observed violent episodes at home. If the child is routinely beaten by parents or has witnessed physical violence between angry adults, he or she will notice how the game is played. Thus, corporal punishment that is not administered according to very carefully thought-out guidelines has the potential to become dangerous. Parenthood does not give the right to slap and intimidate a child because Dad is having a bad day or Mom is in a lousy mood. This kind of unjust discipline causes some well-meaning authorities to reject corporal punishment altogether.

Dobson points out, however, that disciplinary spanking must be distinguished from abusive, harmful forms of corporal punishment. Appropriate disciplinary spanking can play an important role in optimal child development and has been found in prospective studies to be a part of the parenting style associated with the best outcomes. No convincing evidence has been presented that mild spanking is harmful. Indeed, history, research, and a majority of primary care physicians support spanking.

Spanking can and sometimes must be the appropriate response of a parent to a child's defiance. It is not harsh, insulting, dangerous, or whimsical. Rather, it represents the firm but loving discipline that is often in the best interest of the child. How fortunate is the boy or girl whose father and mother still comprehend this timeless concept.

BEFORE YOU BEGIN

1. How do you define the terms *spanking, hitting, beating,* and *abusing?* How are they different, and why do you think corporal punishment has gotten such a bad rap?

2. Why, at times, must a parent administer an appropriate spanking for the child's sake?

3. Under what circumstances would it be wrong for a parent to spank a child?

4. Why is it easier to see the need for a "good spanking" in other children than in your own?

_____

_____

_____

_____

5. What's your personal story with regard to corporal punishment? If you grew up with spankings in the home or at school, what do you remember of those incidents?

_____

_____

_____

_____

LAYING IT OUT

Following are some general principles regarding the loving use of discipline. For more details please refer directly to the complete text of *The New Strong-Willed Child,* chapters 7 and 8.

BIRTH TO SEVEN MONTHS

No *direct* discipline is necessary for a child under seven months of age, regardless of the behavior or circumstance. Many parents do not agree and may swat a child of six months for wiggling while being diapered or for crying at midnight. This is a serious mistake. Why? Because a baby is incapable of comprehending the offense or associating it with the resulting punishment. At this early age, infants need to be held, loved, touched, and soothed with the human voice. They should be fed when hungry and kept clean, dry, and warm. The foundation for emotional and physical health is probably laid during this first six-month period, which should be characterized by security, affection, and warmth.

On the other hand, we can create a fussy, demanding child by rushing to pick up the baby every time he or she utters a whimper or sigh, Dr. Dobson warns. Infants are fully capable of learning to manipulate their parents through a process called reinforcement, whereby any behavior that produces a pleasant result will tend to recur. To avoid this consequence, we need to strike a balance between giving the baby the attention that he or she needs and establishing him or her as a tiny dictator. We shouldn't be afraid to let the baby cry for a reasonable period of time (thought to be healthy for the lungs). We should, though, listen to the tone of the child's voice to determine if he or she is crying because of random discontent or genuine distress. Most parents learn to recognize this distinction very quickly.

EIGHT TO FOURTEEN MONTHS

How do parents discipline a one-year-old? Very carefully and gently. Children at this age are easy to distract and divert. Rather than jerking a china cup from their hands, we should show them a brightly colored alternative—and then be prepared to catch the cup when it falls. When unavoidable confrontations occur, we should win them by firm persistence, not by punishment. Again, we shouldn't be afraid of the child's tears, which can become a potent weapon to avoid naptime or bedtime or a diaper change. We need to have courage to lead the child without being harsh, mean, or gruff.

FIFTEEN TO TWENTY-FOUR MONTHS

This period of life has been called "the first adolescence" because of the negativism, conflict, and defiance of the age. It is a time of excitement over fairy tales, make-believe, and furry puppy dogs. Most important, it is a precious time of loving and warmth that will scurry by all too quickly. Millions of older parents with grown children today would give all they possess to relive those bubbly days with their toddlers.

Dr. Dobson cautions parents not to punish toddlers for behavior that is natural and necessary to learning and development. Exploration of their environment, for example, is of great importance to intellectual stimulation. We look at a crystal trinket and obtain whatever information we seek from that visual inspection. Toddlers, however, will expose it to all their senses. They will pick it up, taste it, smell it, wave it in the air, pound it on the wall, throw it across the room, and listen to the pretty sound it makes when shattering. By that process, they learn a bit about gravity, rough versus smooth surfaces, the brittle nature of glass, and some startling things about their parent's anger. Children at this age must have the freedom to explore their world.

TWO TO THREE YEARS OF AGE

Perhaps the most frustrating aspect of raising children between two and three is their tendency to spill things, destroy things, eat horrible things, fall off things, flush things, kill things, and get into things. They also have a knack for embarrassing actions, like sneezing on the man seated near them at a restaurant. During the toddler years, any unexplained silence of more than thirty seconds can throw an adult into a sudden state of panic.

We *must* keep a sense of humor during the twos and threes in order to preserve our sanity. But we must also proceed with the task of instilling obedience and respect for authority. Thus, most of the comments written in the preceding section also apply to the child between twenty-four and thirty-six months of age. Although the older toddler is much different physically and emotionally than he or she was at eighteen months, the tendency to test and challenge parental authority is still very much in evidence. In fact, when young toddlers consistently win the early confrontations and conflicts, they become even more difficult to handle in the second and third years. Then a lifelong disrespect for authority often begins to settle into their young minds. For their own sakes, this must be avoided.

FOUR TO EIGHT YEARS

By the time a child reaches four years of age, the focus of discipline should not only be on his or her behavior, but also on the *attitudes* motivating the behavior. The task of shaping this expression of the personality can be relatively simple or incredibly difficult, depending on the basic temperament of a particular child. Some youngsters are naturally warm, loving, and trusting, while others sincerely believe the world is out to get them. Some enjoy giving and sharing, while their siblings may be selfish and demanding. Some smile throughout the day, while others complain about everything from toothpaste to broccoli.

Furthermore, these attitudinal patterns are not consistent from one time to the next. They tend to alternate cyclically between rebellion and obedience. Dr. Dobson has found that a time of intense conflict and defiance (if properly handled) will give way to a period of love and cooperation. Then, just as Mom and Dad relax and congratulate themselves for doing a super job of parenting, their little chameleon changes colors again. If it hasn't already, it *will* happen to you.

NINE TO TWELVE YEARS

Ideally, a foundation has been laid during the first nine years that will then permit a general loosening of the lines of authority. This is the ultimate goal, Dobson says. Every year that passes should bring fewer rules, less direct discipline, and more independence for the child. This does not mean that a ten-year-old is suddenly emancipated; it does mean that the child should be permitted to make more decisions about daily living than when he or she was six. It also means that the child should be carrying more responsibility each year of his or her life. Parents must be willing to start letting go.

The overall objective during this final preadolescent period is to teach the child that his or her actions have inevitable consequences. One of the most serious casualties in a permissive society, Dr. Dobson believes, is the failure to connect those two factors: behavior and consequences. How does one connect behavior with consequences? Parents must be willing to let children experience a reasonable amount of pain when they behave irresponsibly. When Craig misses the school bus through his own dawdling, let him walk a mile or two and enter school in midmorning (unless safety factors prohibit this). If Caitlin carelessly loses her lunch money, let her skip a meal. Obviously, it is possible to carry this principle too far, being harsh and inflexible with an immature child. But the best approach is to expect boys and girls to carry the responsibility that is appropriate for their age and occasionally to taste the bitter fruit that irresponsibility bears. That's the only way they'll ever grow up.

THINKING IT THROUGH

1. When might a parent worry too much about his or her baby? When would it be appropriate to let a child less than six months old cry for a time?

_____

_____

_____

_____

2. When reflecting on your child(ren), what would you say has been the most delightful stage of development? What has been the most difficult stage? Explain.

_____

_____

_____

_____

3. How have you taught your children the connection between actions and consequences? What surefire techniques have you learned over the years?

_____

_____

_____

_____

4. When have you experienced the "rebellion-obedience" cycle? Why is this so frustrating for parents?

_____

_____

_____

_____

5. What can a parent do to avoid negativism and bad attitudes in (and toward) a strong-willed child?

_____

_____

_____

_____

CASE STUDY:
Spanking Thanks

Here's an example of corporal punishment administered correctly and with the desired result. William Jarnagin, a father and certified public accountant, wrote the following letter. His story speaks volumes about the proper approach to parent-child relationships.

Dear Dr. Dobson:
This is a note of thanks for your work in strengthening the American family. My wife and I have recently read four of your books and we have profited very much from them.

Please permit me to relate a recent experience with our six-year-old son, David. Last Friday night, my wife, Becky, told him to pick up some orange peelings he had left on the carpet, which he knows is a "no-no." He failed to respond, and as a result received one slap on his behind, whereupon he began an obviously defiant temper tantrum.

Since I had observed the whole episode, I then called for my paddle and applied it appropriately, saw to it that he picked up and properly disposed of the orange peelings, and sent him straight to bed, since it was already past his bedtime. After a few minutes, when his emotions had had a chance to settle down, I went to his room and explained that God had instructed all parents who truly love their children to properly discipline them, etc., and that we truly love him and therefore would not permit such defiant behavior.

The next morning, after I had gone to work, David presented his mother with the following letter, together with a little stack of ten pennies:

From David and Deborah
To Mom and Dad
Ross Dr. 3d house
Sellmer, Tennasse
39718
Dear Mom and Dad
here is 10 Cints for
Pattelling me when I
really neded and that
gos for Deborah to I
love you
Love yur son David
and yur Doter Deborah

Oh, incidentally, Deborah is our one-year-old daughter whose adoption should be final sometime in June.

Keep up your good work and may God bless you.

Sincerely,
William H. Jarnagin

POINTS TO PONDER

1. What is your reaction to this correspondence?

2. At what point do most children become grateful for being disciplined?

3. How effective have you found praying with a child after administering discipline?

4. What are your greatest fears about spanking—and not spanking? Explain your concerns.

Digging Deeper

Any discussion of parental authority and childhood obedience must begin with Ephesians 6:1: "Children, obey your parents in the Lord, for this is right." Parents need to help their children understand that obedience will help protect them from dangers—both external and internal.

In the context of our scriptural study, let's consider two concerns about our children: bad attitudes and lying.

When it comes to the former, there is no substitute for our modeling the attitudes we wish to teach. Someone wrote, "The footsteps a child follows are most likely to be the ones his parents thought they covered up." It is true, Dr. Dobson says. Our children are watching us carefully, and they instinctively imitate our behavior. We can hardly expect them, therefore, to be kind and giving if we are consistently grouchy and selfish. We will be unable to teach appreciativeness if we never say please or thank you at home or away from home. We will not produce honest children if we teach them to lie over the phone to someone trying to collect payment from us by saying, "Dad's not home." In these matters, our boys and girls quickly discern the gap between what we say and what we do. And of the two choices, they usually identify with our behavior and ignore our empty proclamations.

Dr. Dobson has found most of the favorable attitudes that should be taught are actually extrapolations of the Judeo-Christian ethic, including honesty, respect, kindness, love, human dignity, obedience, responsibility, and reverence. How are these time-honored principles conveyed to the next generation? Moses provided the answer more than three thousand years ago in the book of Deuteronomy: "These commandments that I give you today are to be upon your hearts. Impress them on your children. Talk about them when you sit at home and when you walk along the road, when you lie down and when you get up. Tie them as symbols on your hands and bind them on your foreheads. Write them on the doorframes of your houses and on your gates" (Deuteronomy 6:6-9).

Dr. Dobson believes, however, that this training is a constant process. We can't instill these attitudes during a brief, two-minute bedtime prayer or during formal training sessions. We must *live* them from morning to night. They should be reinforced during our casual conversation, which we punctuate with illustrations, demonstrations, compliments, and chastisement.

Lying is another problem every parent must deal with. All children distort the truth from time to time; some even become inveterate liars. Responding appropriately is a task that requires an understanding of child development and the characteristics of the particular individual.

Dr. Dobson would first advise parents to understand that a young child may or may not fully comprehend the difference between lies and the truth. A very thin line stands between fantasy and reality in the mind of a preschool boy or girl. So before we react in a heavy-handed manner, we should be sure to know the child's understanding and intent.

For those children who are clearly lying to avoid unpleasant consequences or to gain an advantage of some sort, parents need to use that circumstance as a teachable moment. Dr. Dobson says the greatest emphasis should be given to telling the truth in all situations. It is a virtue that should be taught—not just when a lie has occurred, but at other times as well. In our devotions with the children, we can read Proverbs 6:16-19 together: "There are six things the LORD hates, seven that are detestable to him: haughty eyes, a lying tongue, hands that shed innocent blood, a heart that devises wicked schemes, feet that are quick to rush into evil, a false witness who pours out lies and a man who stirs up dissension among brothers."

We should explain to the child that in a list of seven things the Lord hates most, two of them deal with dishonesty. Telling the truth is something God cares about; therefore it should matter to us. This will explain why we insist that the son or daughter learn to tell the truth even when it hurts to do so. Our goal should be to lay a foundation that will help us underscore a commitment to honesty in the future.

Of course, we can undermine everything we're trying to establish if we are dishonest in front of our kids. They will note it and behave likewise. If Daddy can twist the truth, he'll have little authority in preventing his kids from doing the same.

POINTS TO PONDER

1. In what areas do you find it easiest to walk your talk? Which are the most difficult for you?

_____

_____

_____

2. When have you allowed your bad attitudes to get the best of you to the detriment of your children? How about little white lies? What kind of example for honesty are you setting?

_____

_____

_____

3. What do you do to share your beliefs, faith, and morals with your children? How do they know you love God?

_____

_____

_____

4. Besides attitude issues and lying, what other concerns do you have about your child's behavior? What Bible verses have you found that you can use to urge your children to take the moral path?

_____

_____

_____

_____

5. When have you spent time talking with your children about the reasons behind the rules? What simple illustrations or resources have you found especially helpful?

_____

_____

_____

_____

TAKING IT HOME

CORPORAL PUNISHMENT AND THE STRONG-WILLED CHILD

Considering his lifelong commitment to the welfare of children, we may wonder why Dr. Dobson recommends corporal punishment as a management tool. He says this is a good question, especially in view of the many articles and editorials appearing in the media these days that resoundingly condemn its use. Convincing the public that corporal punishment is universally harmful has become an unrelenting crusade within certain elements of the media. Dr. Dobson believes their efforts have been terribly misguided.

To put it boldly, he believes that corporal punishment, when used properly, is in children's best interest. Strong-willed boys and girls can be terribly irritating to their parents, as everyone knows. Most of them have figured out how to press all the buttons to make their moms and dads absolutely furious. One father said that nothing in his adult experience could make him angrier than the day-after-day rebellious behavior of his ten-year-old son. Given that kind of volatile interaction, Dr. Dobson is convinced that a determined, hard-nosed kid in the hands of an immature or emotionally unstable parent is a recipe for disaster. The likelihood of physical damage to that youngster is enormous, and it becomes even greater if the parents have been stripped of the ability to control challenging behavior before it gets out of hand.

How much better, and safer, it is for moms and dads to administer a judicious and carefully measured spanking to a child (or even a well-timed swat or two), before she and her parents are both out of control. It is even more advantageous for a savvy strong-willed child to know that spanking is an option, leading the child to back off before he or she goes too far. By depriving parents of this possibility, well-meaning counselors and psychologists inadvertently set up tough-minded kids for disaster at home.

Dr. Dobson has been asked if spanking a child for disobedience sometimes fails. Here was his response.

> Children are so tremendously variable that it is sometimes hard to believe that they are all members of the same human family. Some kids can be crushed with nothing more than a stern look; others seem to require strong and even painful disciplinary measures to make a vivid impression. This difference usually results from the degree to which a child needs adult approval and acceptance. The primary parental task is to see things as the child perceives them, thereby tailoring the discipline to the child's unique needs. Accordingly, it is appropriate to punish a boy or girl when he or she knows it is deserved.
>
> Disciplinary measures usually fail because of fundamental errors in their application. It is possible for twice the amount of punishment to yield half the results. I have made a study of situations in which parents have told me that their children disregard punishment and continue to misbehave. There are four basic reasons for this lack of success:

1. The most common error is whimsical discipline. When the rules change every day and when punishment for misbehavior is capricious and inconsistent, the effort to change behavior is undermined. There is no inevitable consequence to be anticipated. This entices children to see if they can beat the system. In society at large, it also encourages criminal behavior among those who believe they will not face the bar of justice.

2. Sometimes a child is more strong-willed than his parent—and they both know it. He just might be tough enough to realize that a confrontation with his mom or dad is really a struggle of wills. If he can withstand the pressure and not buckle during a major battle, he can eliminate that form of punishment as a tool in the parent's repertoire. Does he think through this process on a conscious level? Usually not, but he understands it intuitively. He realizes that a spanking *must not* be allowed to succeed. Thus, he stiffens his little neck and guts it out. He may even refuse to cry and may say, "That didn't hurt." The parent concludes in exasperation, "Spanking doesn't work for my child."

3. The spanking may be too gentle. If it doesn't hurt, it doesn't motivate a child to avoid the consequence next time. A slap with the hand on the bottom of a diapered two-year-old is not a deterrent to anything. Be sure the child gets the message—while being careful not to go too far.

4. For a few children, spankings are simply not effective. A child who has attention deficit/hyperactivity disorder (ADHD), for example, may be even more wild and unmanageable after corporal punishment. Also, a child who has been abused may identify loving discipline with past abuse. Finally, the very sensitive child might need a different approach. Let me emphasize once more that children are unique. The only way to raise them correctly is to understand each boy or girl as an individual and design parenting techniques to fit the needs and characteristics of that particular child.

POINTS TO PONDER

1. How do your parents, friends, doctors, and others feel about your discipline decisions? From what quarter do you find the most—and least—support?

_____

_____

_____

_____

2. Do you think spanking teaches children that it's okay to hit? Why or why not?

_____

_____

_____

_____

3. When have you felt angry to the point of being out of control? What did you do to avoid a blowup?

_____

_____

_____

_____

4. Do you believe corporal punishment will eventually be outlawed in the United States? Would that really prevent abuse, the main reason cited for such an initiative? Explain your response.

_____

_____

_____

_____

5. How can loving discipline prevent delinquency?

_____

_____

_____

_____

JOURNALING

1. In a perfect world, parents wouldn't have to resort to discipline to get children to obey. Is punishing a child difficult or easy for you? Why?

_____

_____

_____

_____

2. If you are in a two-parent family, are you the tough one or the soft touch when it comes to matters of discipline? How do you feel about your role? List some ways you and your spouse could present a more unified front. If you are a single parent, explain the unique difficulties you face in disciplining your children.

_____

_____

_____

_____

3. What external factors (stress, illness, etc.) could contribute to the problems you're facing with your children?

_____

_____

_____

_____

4. What evidence do you have that your child may even be more strong-willed than you? How does this impact your parent-child roles?

_____

_____

_____

_____

5. Write out a prayer listing the attributes and attitudes you hope to see develop in your children. List ways to encourage such positive behaviors.

_____

_____

_____

_____

7

SIBLING RIVALRY

Taken from chapter 9, "Bitter Brothers & Surly Sisters"

GETTING IT STARTED

If parents were asked to indicate the most irritating feature of child rearing, Dr. Dobson is convinced that sibling rivalry would win hands down. He says, "It has the capacity of driving otherwise sane and self-controlled adults a little crazy. Children are not content just to hate each other in private. They attack one another like miniature warriors, mobilizing their troops and probing for a weakness in the defensive line. They argue, hit, kick, scream, grab, taunt, tattle, and sabotage the opposing forces. I knew one child who deeply resented being sick with a cold while his older sibling was healthy, so he secretly blew his nose on the mouthpiece of his brother's clarinet! The big losers from such combat, of course, are the harassed parents who must listen to the noise of the battlefield and then try to patch up the wounded."

Dr. Dobson teaches some valuable lessons about siblings and how they interact with one another from an elementary principle of physics: a hot object will gradually raise the temperature of a cooler one nearby. His point is that a rebellious child usually makes the compliant youngster harder to handle. That is especially true if the strong-willed child is older. Parents often find that their fun-loving, go-along-to-get-along boy or girl starts to pick up the aggres-

111

sive attitudes and behavior of the tougher brother or sister. In fact, every member of a family can be influenced by a particularly difficult youngster, usually for the worse.

BEFORE YOU BEGIN

1. When have you experienced your compliant, kindly kids being influenced and led astray by strong-willed friends or sibling(s)?

_____

_____

_____

2. What are some of the more devastating examples you've seen of sibling rivalry? How did it play out between you and your siblings?

_____

_____

_____

3. What can parents do proactively to defuse competition between children? Conversely, how might parents make matters worse?

_____

_____

_____

4. What negative traits do you see in strong-willed children you know? How would you respond if those characteristics began to appear in your child?

_____

_____

_____

_____

5. What can you do to embolden a compliant child to stand up for what's right and avoid being bullied?

_____

_____

_____

_____

LAYING IT OUT

Dr. Dobson has created a practical plan of action for parents who want to combat the poison of sibling rivalry. Here are his suggestions.

1. Don't inflame the natural jealousy of children

Sibling rivalry is a virtual inevitability, especially between strong-willed kids, but Mom and Dad should at least seek to avoid situations that make it worse. One of these is comparing children unfavorably with each other, since they are always looking for a competitive edge. The question in a child's mind is not, "How am I doing?" It is, "How am I doing compared to my brother or sister?" The issue is not how fast a child can run but who crosses the finish line first. A boy does not care how tall he is but who is tallest. Children systematically measure themselves against their peers on everything from skateboarding ability to having the most friends. Accordingly, parents who want a little peace at home should guard against comparative comments that routinely favor one child over another. To violate this principle is to set up even greater rivalry between the two.

Precipitating a fight between children is easy. All that is necessary is to toss a treat in the direction of one of them and then step back and watch them fight over it. This can be done by repeating negative comments made by one about the other or by baiting the first in the presence of the second. It can be accomplished in business by assigning similar territory to two managers. They will tear each other to pieces in the places where their responsibilities overlap.

Children and teens are particularly uptight about physical attractiveness and body characteristics. Commending one child at the expense of the other can be highly inflammatory. Suppose, for example, that Rachel is permitted to hear this casual remark about her sister: "Becky sure is going to be a gorgeous girl." The very fact that Rachel was not mentioned will probably establish the two girls as rivals. If the two vary significantly in beauty, we can be sure that Rachel has already concluded, *Yeah, I'm the ugly one.* When her peers confirm her fears, she feels resentful and jealous.

Intelligence is another hot button for children. Often parents say in front of their children, "I think Alissa is actually brighter than Mark." How foolish! Here comes another battle. Adults sometimes find it difficult to comprehend how powerful that kind of comparison can be in a child's mind. Even when the comments are unplanned and spoken offhandedly, they convey how a child is seen within the family. Everyone is vulnerable to the power of that bit of information.

2. Establish a workable system of justice at home

Sibling rivalry is also at its worst when inadequate or inconsistently applied rules govern the interaction between kids—when the "lawbreakers" do not get caught, or, if apprehended, are set free without standing trial. We need to understand that society establishes and enforces laws in order to protect people from each other.

Individual families are similar to societies in their need for law and order. In the absence of justice, "neighboring" siblings begin to assault one another. The older child is bigger and tougher, which allows him or her to oppress younger brothers and sisters. But the junior member of the family is not without weapons. This child can strike back by breaking the toys and prized possessions of the older sibling and interfering when friends are visiting. Mutual hatred then erupts like an angry volcano, spewing its destructive contents on everyone in its path.

Too often, however, children who appeal to their parents for intervention are left to fight it out among themselves. Mom or Dad may not have sufficient disciplinary control to enforce their judgments. In some families, they can become so exasperated with the constant bickering among siblings that they refuse to get involved. In others, they require an older child to live with an admitted injustice "because your sister is smaller than you." Thus, they tie the older child's hands and render him or her utterly defenseless against the mischief of the younger sibling. And in the many families today in which both parents work, the children may be busily disassembling each other at home with no supervision whatsoever.

One of the most important responsibilities of parents, says Dr. Dobson, is to establish an equitable system of justice and a balance of power at home. Reasonable rules should be enforced fairly for each member of the family. While they can never be implemented perfectly, the following will give parents a place to start:

⋆ A child is *never* allowed to make fun of the other in a destructive way. Period! This must be an inflexible rule with no exceptions.

⋆ Each child's room is his or her private territory. Doors must have locks, and permission to enter is a revocable privilege. (Families with more than one child in each bedroom can allocate available living space for each youngster.)

⋆ As much as possible, the older child is not permitted to tease the younger child.

⋆ The younger child is forbidden from harassing the older child.

⋆ The children are not required to play with each other when they prefer to be alone or with other friends.

⋆ Parents mediate any genuine conflict as quickly as possible, being careful to show impartiality and extreme fairness.

As with any system of justice, this plan requires (1) respect for leadership of the parents, (2) willingness of the parents to mediate, (3) reasonable consistency over time, and (4) occasional enforcement or punishment. Dr. Dobson has found that when this approach is accomplished with love, the emotional tone of the home can be changed from one of hatred to (at least) tolerance.

3. Recognize that the hidden "target" of sibling rivalry is you

The third general principle is a matter of understanding how kids think. Their conflict often becomes a way of manipulating parents. Quarreling and fighting provide an opportunity for both children to capture adult attention. It has been written, "Some children had rather be wanted for murder than not wanted at all." Toward this end, a pair of obnoxious kids can tacitly agree to bug their parents until they get a response—even if it is an angry reaction.

One father told Dr. Dobson about the time his son and his nephew began to argue and then beat each other with their fists. Both fathers were nearby and decided to let the fight run its natural course. During the first lull in the action, one of the boys glanced sideways toward the passive men and said, "Isn't anybody going to stop us before we get hurt?" The fight, you see, was something neither boy wanted. Their violent combat was directly related to the presence of the two adults and would have taken a different form if the boys had been alone. Children will "hook" their parents' attention and intervention in this way.

Believe it or not, this form of sibling rivalry is easiest to control. The parents must simply render the behavior unprofitable to each participant. Dr. Dobson recommends that parents review the problem (for example, a morning full of bickering) with the children and then say, "Now, listen carefully. If the two of you want to pick on each other and make yourselves miserable, then be my guests" (assuming there is a fairly equal balance of power between them). "Go outside and argue until you're exhausted. But it's not going to occur under my feet anymore. It's over! And you know that I mean business when I make that kind of statement. Do we understand each other?"

Having made the boundaries clear, Dobson believes decisive action is required the instant either child returns to his bickering. If the children had separate bedrooms, he would confine one child to each room for at least thirty minutes of complete boredom without radio, computer, or television. Or he'd assign one to clean the garage and the other to mow the lawn. Or he'd make them both take an unscheduled nap. Dr. Dobson's purpose would be to make the children understand that the parent is serious the next time Mom or Dad asks for peace and tranquility.

Children must not be permitted to destroy the joy of living. And what is most surprising is that children are the happiest when their parents enforce reasonable limits with love and dignity. It takes work, but it can be done.

THINKING IT THROUGH

1. What do you think of Dr. Dobson's list of rules for harmony in the home? Which ones could you add to your home to make it more peaceful?

_____

_____

_____

2. What would be the result if parents eliminated all aspects of individuality within family life so no one had his or her feelings hurt?

_____

_____

_____

3. How do you make sure that in matters of beauty, brains, athletic ability, and anything else valued in the family or neighborhood, your children know they are respected and have equal worth with their siblings?

4. What are some ways you've succeeded at evenly distributing praise and criticism? What are some ways you've fallen short?

5. When have you seen your child building a fortress around a weakness? What is it that your child fears or thinks he or she is poor at? What can you do when you see the signals (bragging or boasting) that indicate your child is in need of a hug and a compliment?

6. What are some creative punishments you might devise to ensure that noncooperative siblings get along better?

_____

_____

_____

CASE STUDY:
Jealous Siblings

Dear Jim:

I am the greatest and your the badest. And I can beat everybody in a race and you can't beat anybody in a race. I'm the smartest and your the dumbest. I'm the best sport player and your the badest sport player. And your also a hog. I can beat anybody up. And that's the truth. And that's the end of this story.

Yours truly,
Richard

Children (especially teens) also can be extremely competitive with regard to physical attributes and athletic abilities. Those who are slower, weaker, and less coordinated than their brothers or sisters are rarely able to accept second best with grace and dignity. Consider, for example, the above note. It was written by a nine-year-old to his eight-year-old brother the evening after the younger child had beaten him in a race.

Dr. Dobson found the note from little Richard humorous because his motive was so poorly disguised. He had been badly stung by his humiliation on the field of honor, so he came home and raised the battle flags. He probably spent the next eight weeks looking for opportunities to fire torpedoes into Jim's soft underbelly. Such is the nature of humankind.

POINTS TO PONDER

1. How aware are you of the strengths and weaknesses, power and pain in your children's lives? What do you do to encourage your children to grow in their areas of obvious skill? How do you go about finding latent interests and abilities?

2. What would you have said to Richard if the note had been directed to your son? How do you think it made Jim feel?

3. What are the positive elements of competition? In what ways can competition be unhealthy?

4. How can you teach a child it's okay to come in second? What are some strategies for teaching a child how to lose gracefully?

_____

_____

_____

_____

DIGGING DEEPER

THE PRODIGAL'S BIG BROTHER

Sibling rivalry is not new. It was responsible for the first murder on record (when Cain killed Abel) and has been present in virtually every home with more than one child from that time to now. Dr. Dobson says that the underlying source of this conflict is old-fashioned jealousy and competition between children.

The consequences of such inequity should be obvious. Even though the compliant child usually goes along with the program and does not complain, he or she may accumulate a volume of resentment through the years. Isn't that what seems to have occurred to the brother of the Prodigal Son, as described by Jesus in the book of Luke 15:11-32? The older brother was the hardworking, responsible, compliant member of the family. Apparently, his kid brother was irresponsible, flighty, and strong-willed. Extrapolating a bit from the biblical account, Dobson notes that little love seems to be lost between these sons, even before the prodigal's impulsive departure.

He retells the story this way:

> The self-disciplined elder brother resented the spoiled brat who got everything he asked for. Nevertheless, the older brother kept his thoughts to himself. He would not want to upset his father, whom he respected

enormously. Then came that incredible day when little brother demanded his entire inheritance in one lump sum. The compliant son overheard the conversation and gasped in shock. *What audacity!* he thought. Then, to his amazement he heard his father grant the playboy's request. He could hear the clink of numerous gold coins being counted. The elder brother was furious. We can only assume that the departure of this sibling meant Big Bud would have to handle double chores and work longer hours in the fields. It wasn't fair that the load should fall on him. Nevertheless, he said nothing. Compliant people are inclined to hold their feelings inside, but they are capable of harboring great resentment.

The years passed slowly as the elder brother labored to maintain the farm. The father had grown older by then, placing a heavier strain on this firstborn son. Every day he labored from dawn to dusk in the hot sun. Occasionally, he thought about his brother living it up in the far country, and he was briefly tempted. But, no. He would do what was right. Pleasing his father was the most important thing in his life.

Then, as we remember, the strong-willed goof-off ran out of money and became exceedingly hungry. He thought of his mom's cooking and the warmth of his father's fire. He clutched his rags around him and began the long journey home. When he was yet afar off, his father ran to meet him—embracing him and placing the royal robes around his shoulders. The fatted calf was killed and a great feast planned. That did it. The compliant brother could take no more. The Prodigal Son had secured through his folly what the elder brother could not gain through his discipline: the approval and affection of his father. His spirit was wounded!

Whether Dr. Dobson's interpretation of this parable is faithful to the meaning of the Scripture will be left to the theologians. He is certain of one thing: Strong-willed and compliant siblings have played out this drama since the days of Cain and Abel, and the responsible brother or sister often feels like the loser. This sibling holds his or her feelings inside and then pays a price for storing them. He or she is more susceptible as an adult to ulcers, hypertension, colitis, migraine headaches, and a wide range of other psychosomatic illnesses. Furthermore, the responsible brother or sister's sense of utter powerlessness can drive his or her anger underground. It may emerge in less obvious quests for control. It is not necessary or healthy to allow children to destroy each other and make life miserable for the adults around them. Sibling rivalry is difficult to cure, but it certainly can be treated.

POINTS TO PONDER

1. Dr. Dobson believes the Prodigal Son's older brother had a wounded spirit. How could the boy's father have been more sensitive to his compliant son's feelings? How do you think the two brothers resolved their problems?

_____

_____

_____

2. How do you know if your child is harboring resentment toward his or her siblings? What are some ways you can get the quiet child to open up?

_____

_____

_____

3. Dr. Dobson has a tender heart for single parents. What single-parent families do you know? What are some simple, practical ways you could help them out?

_____

_____

_____

4. What are some unique concerns single parents face that two-parent families don't worry about? What are some universal concerns shared by all parents?

_____

_____

_____

_____

5. If you have a prodigal child, what circumstances prompted the severed relationship? What are you actively doing to seek reconciliation?

_____

_____

_____

_____

TAKING IT HOME

PRACTICAL SIBLING CONCERNS

When asked about the wisdom of spacing the birth of children, Dr. Dobson noted that children who are two years apart and of the same sex are more likely to be competitive with each other. On the other hand, Dr. Dobson says, they are also more likely to enjoy mutual companionship. If your babies are four or more years apart, they will experience less camaraderie, but you'll at least have only one child in college at a time. Dr. Dobson points out that there are many more important reasons for planning a baby at a particular time than the age of those already born. Of greater significance are the health of the mother, the parents' desire for another child, financial considerations, and the stability of the marriage. The relative age of the siblings is not one of the major determiners, in his opinion.

Dr. Dobson once responded to a letter from a mom whose older child was a great student earning straight A's year after year. Her younger sister, however, was completely bored in school and wouldn't even try. The frustrating thing, said the mother, was that the younger girl is probably brighter than her older sister. The mother asked why her daughter would refuse to apply her abilities like this.

Here's what Dr. Dobson had to say.

> There could be many reasons for your younger daughter's academic disinterest, but let me suggest the most probable explanation. Children will often refuse to compete when they think they are likely to place second instead of first. Therefore, a younger child may avoid challenging an older sibling in her area of greatest strength. If Son Number One is a great athlete, then Son Number Two may be more interested in collecting butterflies. If Daughter Number One is an accomplished pianist, then Daughter Number Two may scorn music and take up tennis. . . . The younger sibling desperately [wants] to do something else in which he [will] not be compared unfavorably. . . . It would be wise to accept something less than perfection from her school performance. Siblings need not fit the same mold—nor can we force them to do so.

With regard to sibling rivalry, another cause of irritation and frustration to parents is the fact that strong-willed and compliant children often resent each other deeply. Dr. Dobson has found that the tougher individuals dislike their prissy siblings who do everything right and are punished far less often. The easy children, on the other hand, get sick and tired of seeing the rebellious sib take on Mom or Dad and often come out the winner. The compliant children are sometimes expected to "just take it" because parents are weary of fighting with (and losing to) the rebellious youngster. The old adage that "the squeaky wheel gets the grease" applies here, Dr. Dobson notes. Strong-willed kids tend to get away with more because they simply never give up and their parents become exasperated just trying to hang in there.

If there is an unpleasant job to be done, the compliant kid will be expected to do it. Mom and Dad just don't have the energy to fight with the tiger. If one child is to be chosen for a pleasant experience, it will probably go to the brattier of the two because he would scream bloody murder if excluded. When circumstances require one child to sacrifice or do without, you know who will be elected. Parents who favor the strong-willed child in this way are aware that they are being unfair, but their sense of justice has yielded to the pressures of practicality. They are simply too depleted and frustrated to risk irritating the tougher kid.

POINTS TO PONDER

1. In what areas do your children tend to compare themselves to one another? How can you encourage them to find value in the way God has created them? What difference has the spacing of children had in your home? What are the advantages and disadvantages to children close in age growing up together?

2. When have you found it easier to reward the little rebel in your family because you feared the fuss he or she would raise? How did this make your other children feel?

3. When you're feeling especially stressed or exhausted, what do you do to recharge?

_____

_____

_____

JOURNALING

1. Write out a prayer for some single parents you know (or yourself if appropriate). Make a concerted effort to connect with and befriend such a family.

_____

_____

_____

2. If you have a prodigal child in your immediate family or know of a friend in such a situation, how can you come alongside them with hope and encouragement? Write out a prayer for that prodigal and his or her parents. Consider ways you can avoid broken relationships in your own home.

_____

_____

_____

3. If appropriate, confess your part in driving a wedge between your children. What are some ways you could help your offspring to be better friends to one another?

_____

_____

_____

_____

4. Write out rules for your family that will help to ensure order and peace in your home. Tailor them to your unique situation and needs.

_____

_____

_____

_____

5. How do you mediate disputes between children? Explore how you might bring prayer and Scripture into these times of growth and correction.

_____

_____

_____

_____

8

THE STRONG-WILLED ADOLESCENT

(Is There Any Other Kind?)

Taken from chapter 10, "The Strong-Willed Adolescent"

GETTING IT STARTED

Adolescence is that dynamic time of life that comes in with a pimple and goes out with a beard—or to put it another way, it comes in with a bicycle and ends with a car. It's an exciting time of life, but to be honest, not something any of us would probably want to repeat. We adults remember all too clearly the fears, jeers, and tears of our tumultuous youth. Perhaps that's why many parents begin to get nervous when their children approach the adolescent years, especially if one of them has been the family troublemaker.

According to Dr. Dobson, one of the curious aspects of the teen experience today, which wasn't true thirty years ago, is its largely homogenized nature around the world. He points out, for example, that adults who have traveled internationally may recognize a certain kind of graffiti spray painted on buildings, bridges, and trains wherever they go. It looks about the same in Sydney, Chicago, London, Moscow, or Berlin. Somehow kids around the world know how to duplicate those scrawled block letters that mark gang territories. Teens in far-flung places busily imitate each other in many other ways. They are determined to look alike, dress alike, and "be" alike wherever they are found. Kids even have their own international language of sorts that adapts to the ever-changing jargon of the moment, Dr. Dobson notes.

What common bond links young people together? It is the worldwide pop culture, which knows no geographical boundaries. MTV, the most watched television cable network in the world, is the primary vehicle driving this conformity. Its wretched twenty-four–hour programming is seen now in more than 377 million households every day, mostly by impressionable teens or young adults. The corporate conglomerate makes billions of dollars marketing pop culture—and rebellion—to a generation. Its executives are not only keenly aware of the influence they are having around the world—that is precisely what they are striving for.

Dr. Dobson says that MTV is not the only degrading cultural force operating on the international scene. The American entertainment industry also shapes the worldwide community negatively through its distribution of movies, television, videos, and the Internet. Parents need to help children to learn to fight against these crushing influences.

BEFORE YOU BEGIN

1. How much time do your children spend watching TV, listening to music, or playing computer and video games? What type of programming do they like? What specifically concerns you?

2. How do you feel about children having a television set, computer, DVD player, or VCR in the bedroom?

3. When's the last time you sat down with your teen, watched a TV program or movie together, and then discussed its message? When have you done this with a favorite song of theirs?

_____

_____

_____

_____

4. In what ways has the culture impacted the way your child thinks, talks, dresses, or buys? Why are adolescents so desperate to conform?

_____

_____

_____

_____

5. What do you do to limit teen spending and ensure good stewardship?

_____

_____

_____

_____

6. In your opinion, when does a child become an adult? Explain.

_____

_____

_____

_____

Laying It Out

The strong-willed adolescent is a unique creature. Dr. Dobson has found these teens much more difficult to tame than their compliant counterparts. He does, however, offer some pointers to help struggling parents.

THE RESPECT THEY DESERVE

Give teenagers the gifts they hunger for most—respect and dignity! We know that early adolescence is typically a painful time of life, marked by rapid physical and emotional changes. Dr. Dobson illustrates this characteristic difficulty in his story of a seventh-grade boy who had been asked to recite Patrick Henry's historic speech at a special program commemorating the birth of the United States.

When the young man stood nervously before an audience of parents, he became confused and blurted out: "Give me puberty or give me death!" His statement is not as ridiculous as it sounds. Many teens sincerely believe they must choose between these dubious alternatives.

The thirteenth and fourteenth years commonly are the most difficult twenty-four months in life. A preadolescent child of ten or twelve suddenly awakens to a brand-new world, as though his or her eyes were opening for the first time. That world is populated by age-mates who frighten him or her.

This young person's greatest anxiety, even exceeding the fear of death (which is remote and unthinkable) is the possibility of rejection or humiliation in the eyes of his or her peers. This ominous threat will lurk in the background for years, motivating kids to do things that make absolutely no sense to the adults who watch. It is impossible to comprehend the adolescent mind without understanding this terror of the peer group.

Related to this social vulnerability are the doubt and feelings of inferiority that reach an all-time high at this age. An adolescent's worth as a human being hangs precariously on peer-group acceptance, which is notoriously fickle. Thus, relatively minor evidences of rejection or ridicule become major to those who already see themselves as fools and failures.

It is difficult to overestimate the impact of having no one to sit with on the school-sponsored field trip, not being invited to an important event, being laughed at by the "in" group, waking up in the morning to find seven shiny new pimples on your oily forehead, or being humiliated by the boy or girl you thought had liked you, says Dr. Dobson. In fact, some adolescents consistently face these kinds of social catastrophes throughout their teen years. It makes some of the most strong-willed ones downright mean at home.

IT'S NOT YOU

Here's the key to the puzzle. There is often an irrationality associated with adolescence that can be terribly frustrating to parents. During that time, parents find great difficulty in reasoning their way out of conflict. They end up holding bizarre conversations with their uncomprehending adolescent. It's as though parents and teenagers come from different planets.

These moments will likely occur while you are trying to explain why he must be home by a certain hour, why she should keep her room straight, why he can't have the car on Friday night, or why it doesn't really matter that she wasn't invited to the cool party given by the most popular kid in the senior class.

These issues defy reason, and teens are more likely to respond instead to the dynamic emotional, social, and chemical forces that propel them. Dr. Dobson has noted, from the survey of thirty-five thousand parents he made to prepare for writing *The Strong-Willed Child,* that strong-willed children are especially susceptible to these internal and sometimes irrational forces. Whatever testiness there was in the past twelve years is likely to get worse before it gets better.

What is going on here? Why the sudden volatility and irrationality? Dr. Dobson asks. The answer is straightforward. It's the mischievous hormones that have begun to surge! They are the key to understanding nearly everything that doesn't add up in the teen years. Dramatic changes are going on inside! These emotional changes are timed to coincide precisely with the onset of physical maturation, driven by a hormonal assault that is common to both. Dobson concludes that human chemistry apparently goes haywire for a few years, affecting mind as much as body.

COMMUNICATE OR ELSE

But how can you talk to someone who won't talk—someone whose language consists of seven phrases: "I dunno," "I don't care," "Leave me alone," "I need money," "Can I have the car?" "My friends think you're unfair," and "I didn't do it"? The situation can be frustrating.

Dr. Dobson explains that prying open the door of communication with an angry adolescent can require more tact and skill than any other parenting assignment. Often, mothers and fathers act like adolescents themselves, shouting, screaming, and engaging in endless battles that leave them exhausted but without strategic advantage. We must have a better way of communicating than shouting at one another. Dr. Dobson proposes an alternative.

Talk even if you're not sure they're listening. Be sure your teen understands the ground rules before you lower the boom. Don't be afraid to say what needs to be said, but neither should you be shocked if your words reach (apparently) deaf ears.

Dr. Dobson has found that an open and honest boy or girl may reveal deep feelings at such a moment of communication, permitting a priceless time of catharsis and ventilation. On the other hand, a stubborn, defiant, proud adolescent may sit immobile with head downward. But even if your teenager remains stoic or hostile, at least the cards have been laid on the table and parental intentions have been explained.

KEEP THEM MOVING

Dr. Dobson also gives a word of practical advice for the parents of very strong-willed adolescents: They simply must not be allowed to get bored. Giving these teenagers large quantities of unstructured time is asking for trouble. The hormones that surge through their youthful bodies, especially testosterone in boys, will often lead them in the direction of danger or trouble, Dr. Dobson warns. That's why unsupervised time after school, when parents are at work, can lead to harmful behavior. The old adage warns, "An idle mind is the devil's workshop." It's true.

Dr. Dobson's advice is to get these energetic, mischievous teenagers occupied in constructive activities (without overdoing it). We should see that they get into a good youth program (from his perspective, a Bible-believing church would be the best place to start) or become involved in sports, music, hobbies, animal care, part-time jobs, or an academic interest such as electronics or agriculture. Obviously, implementing this suggestion is not as urgent for the parents of compliant kids, but the idea is still relevant, Dr. Dobson says. By whatever means, you must find a way to keep their gangly legs churning.

Not only should adolescents be busy in constructive activities, they desperately need personal connectedness to their family. Every available study draws this conclusion. When parents are involved intimately with their teens—including eating together as a family as often as possible—rebellious and destructive behavior is less likely to occur.

USE INCENTIVES AND PRIVILEGES

Dr. Dobson says that one of the most common mistakes parents of rebellious kids make is allowing themselves to be drawn into endless verbal battles that leave them exhausted but without strategic advantage. He warns, "Don't subject your daughter to perpetual threats and finger-wagging accusations and insulting indictments. And most important, don't nag her endlessly. Adolescents hate to be nagged by Mommy and Daddy!"

When that occurs, teenagers typically protect themselves by appearing deaf. Thus, the quickest way to terminate all communication between generations is to follow a young person around the house, repeating the same monotonous messages of disapproval. An adolescent must understand the connection between actions and consequences, responsibilities and privileges. If the teenager fails to live up to his or her end of the bargain, we should revoke a privilege. Conveying this message is a crucial part of a parent's job.

HOLD THEM WITH AN OPEN HAND

Another serious mistake made by parents of older teenagers (sixteen to nineteen years of age) is refusing to grant them the independence and maturity they require. As loving guardians, our inclination is to hold our kids too tightly, despite their attempts to squirm free. Dr. Dobson has seen parents who try to make all their children's decisions, keep them snugly beneath their wings, and prevent even the possibility of failure.

When we do that, we force our young adults into one of two destructive patterns: Either they passively accept our overprotection and remain dependent "children" into adult life, or they rise up in great wrath to reject our bondage and interference. They lose on both counts. On the one hand, they become emotional cripples, incapable of independent thought, and on the other they grow into angry, guilt-ridden adults who have severed ties with the family they need. Indeed, parents who refuse to grant appropriate independence to their older adolescents are courting disaster not only for their children but also for themselves.

Dr. Dobson notes that this process of granting appropriate independence must begin when the child is a toddler and continue throughout the elementary school years. He suggests that parents should permit their kids to go to summer camp even though it might be safer to keep them at home. They should allow them to spend the night with their friend when invited. They should make their own bed, take care of their animals, and do their homework. In short, the parental purpose should be to grant increasing freedom and responsibility year by year, so that when the child gets beyond adult control, he or she will no longer need it.

Our objective as parents, then, should be to do nothing for boys and girls that they can profit from doing for themselves. Dr. Dobson admits the difficulty of implementing this policy because we love our children deeply and are tremendously vulnerable to their needs. Life inevitably brings pain and sorrow to little people, and we hurt when they hurt.

When others ridicule our kids or laugh at them, when they feel lonely and rejected, when they fail at something important, when they cry in the midnight hours, when physical harm threatens their existence—these are the trials that seem unbearable to those of us who watch from the sidelines. Growing up can be painful.

We want to rise like a mighty shield to protect them from life's sting—to hold them snugly within the safety of our embrace. Yet we must let them struggle at times. Children can't grow without taking risks, he says. Toddlers can't walk initially without falling down. Students can't learn without facing some hardships. And ultimately, an adolescent can't enter young adulthood until we release him or her from our protective custody.

THINKING IT THROUGH

1. What traumas do you remember from your days of puberty? What are some of your best memories from that time of life?

_____

_____

_____

_____

2. When have you witnessed an example of irrational adolescent behavior? Share your best war story.

_____

_____

_____

_____

3. What do you see as the greatest barrier to communicating with your teen? What ways have you discovered to get your child to open up?

_____

_____

_____

_____

4. What positive steps have you taken to keep a teen with raging hormones out of trouble? How can you keep them (and yourself) sane?

_____

_____

_____

_____

CASE STUDY:
The Doctor Is In . . . Trouble

Dr. Dobson tells this story:

When I was sixteen years old, I began to play some games that my mother viewed with alarm. I had not yet crossed the line into all-out rebellion, but I was definitely leaning in that direction. My father was a minister who traveled constantly during that time, and Mom was in charge. One night, we had an argument over a dance I wanted to go to, and she objected. I openly defied her that night. I said, in effect, that I was going and if she didn't like it, that was just too bad. Mom became very quiet, and I turned in a huff to go into my bedroom. I paused in the hall when I heard her pick up the phone and call my dad, who was out of town. She simply said, "I need you." What happened in the next few days shocked me down to my toes. My dad canceled his four-year speaking schedule and put our house up for sale. Then he accepted a pastoral assignment seven hundred miles south. The next thing I knew, I was on a train heading for Texas and a new home in the Rio Grande Valley. That permitted my dad to be at home with me for my last two years of high school. During these years we hunted and fished together and bonded for a lifetime. There in a fresh environment, I made new friends and worked my way through the conflict that was brewing with my mom. I didn't fully understand until later the price my parents paid to do what was best for me. It was a very costly move for them, personally and professionally, but they loved me enough to sacrifice at a critically important time. In essence, they saved me. I was moving in the wrong direction, and they pulled me back from the cliff. I will always appreciate these good people for what they did.

POINTS TO PONDER

1. For couples: How do you show your support for each other? For single parents: How can other people in the church give you support and assistance?

2. Why was it so important for Dr. Dobson's father to put his son before his career? What are some ways you've done this very thing for your children?

3. Consider the lifelong impact of the bonding between Dr. Dobson and his father and mother. How are you making lasting memories with your children today?

_____

_____

_____

_____

4. How do you typically respond to open defiance from your teen? Share examples and solutions.

_____

_____

_____

_____

DIGGING DEEPER

Parents have no role more vital than introducing their children to Jesus Christ and then grounding them thoroughly in the principles of the faith. Dr. Dobson says this is job #1.

Everything of value depends on one primary responsibility—that of providing our kids with an unshakable faith in Jesus Christ. How can anything else compare to the significance of keeping the family circle unbroken in the life to come? Dr. Dobson asks. What an incredible objective to work toward!

If the salvation of our children is really that vital to us, then our spiritual training should begin before children can even comprehend what it is all about. They should grow up seeing their parents on their knees before God, talking to Him. Children learn quickly at that age and will never forget what they've seen and heard. Even if our kids reject their faith later, the seeds planted during that time will be with them for the rest of their lives. This is why we are instructed to "bring them up in the nurture and admonition of the Lord" (Ephesians 6:4, KJV).

Not every child responds early or dramatically to the gospel message, nor should he or she be expected to. Some are more sensitive to spiritual matters than others, and each one must be allowed to progress at his or her own pace. But in no sense should we parents be casual or neutral about our children's training. Their world should sparkle with references to Jesus and to our faith.

That is the meaning of Deuteronomy 6:6-9: "These commandments that I give you today are to be upon your hearts. Impress them on your children. Talk about them when you sit at home and when you walk along the road, when you lie down and when you get up. Tie them as symbols on your hands and bind them on your foreheads. Write them on the doorframes of your houses and on your gates." Scripture should be a part of their daily lives.

Dr. Dobson remembers his mother reading the story of Samson to him when he was nine years old. After this mighty warrior fell into sin, you will recall, the Philistines gouged out his eyes and held him as a common slave. Some time later, Samson repented before God and was forgiven. He was even given back his awesome strength. But Dr. Dobson's mother pointed out that Samson never regained his eyesight, nor did he ever live in freedom again. He and his enemies died together as the temple collapsed upon them.

Dr. Dobson has found that many parents would not agree with his mother's decision to acquaint him with the nature of sin and its consequences. They might say, "Oh, I wouldn't want to paint such a negative picture for my kids. I want them to think of God as a loving Father, not as a wrathful judge who punishes us." In so doing, they withhold a portion of the truth from their children. God is both perfect love and perfect judgment. In 116 places throughout the Bible, we are told to "fear the Lord."

It's impossible to overstate the importance of teaching divine accountability, especially to our strong-willed children. Since their tendency is to test the limits and break the rules, they will need this internal standard to guide their behavior. Although not all will listen to it, some will. But while doing that we should be careful to balance the themes of love and justice as we teach our children about

God. To tip the scales in either direction would be to distort the truth and create confusion in a realm where understanding is of utmost significance.

POINTS TO PONDER

1. How do we fail our children by emphasizing only the benevolent side of God to the exclusion of His wrath and judgment? Why must our presentation of the nature of God be balanced?

2. How would you convey the reality of God's moral laws to a teen? What image or example might help you get the point across?

3. In what ways do you personally prepare for the divine accountability of Judgment Day? How are you getting your child ready for that great day?

4. What effective approaches have you used to help you teach your children about the gospel? How do you take into account the fact that each child comes to Christ uniquely?

_____

_____

_____

_____

TAKING IT HOME

In closing, Dr. Dobson offers THREE guidelines for parenting efforts during the final era of childhood: adolescence.

1. Hold on with an open hand.

This implies that we still care about the outcome during early adulthood, but we must not clutch our children too tightly. Our grip must be relaxed. We should pray for them, love them, and even offer advice to them when it is sought. But the responsibility to make personal decisions must be borne by the next generation, and they must also accept the consequences of those choices.

2. Hold them close and let them go.

This seven-word suggestion could almost represent the theme of Dr. Dobson's book. Parents should be deeply involved in the lives of their young children, providing love, protection, and authority, Dr. Dobson says. But when those children reach their late teens and early twenties, the cage door must be opened to the world outside.

That, according to Dr. Dobson, is the most frightening time of parenthood, particularly for Christian mothers and fathers who care so deeply about the spiritual welfare of their families. How difficult it is to await an answer to the question, "Did I train them properly?" The tendency is to retain control in an attempt to avoid hearing the wrong reply to that all-important question. Nevertheless, our sons and daughters are more likely to make proper choices when they do not have to rebel against our meddling interference in order to gain their independence.

3. If you love something, set it free. If it comes back to you, then it's yours. If it doesn't return, then it was never yours in the first place.

Dr. Dobson says this little aphorism contains great wisdom. Love demands freedom. This is true not only of relationships between animals and humans but also of all interpersonal interactions. For example, the quickest way to destroy romantic love between a husband and wife is for one partner to clamp a steel cage around the other.

Dr. Dobson has seen hundreds of women trying unsuccessfully to demand love and fidelity from their husbands. It doesn't work. Think back to your dating experiences before marriage. Do you recall that any romantic relationship was doomed the moment one partner began to worry about losing the other, phoning six or eight times a day and hiding behind trees to see who was competing for the lover's attention? That hand-wringing performance will devastate a perfectly good love relationship in a matter of days. To repeat: *Love demands freedom*. Don't be afraid to offer it to your children.

POINTS TO PONDER

1. What will be the most difficult aspect for you of setting your child free one day? Who will have a tougher time—you or your spouse?

2. What can you do to pray more for and with your children?

_____

_____

_____

_____

3. When you see the changeable behavior in your adolescent, what is your initial response? Talk about a situation in which you reacted too quickly and paid a price relationally. Then tell one of your success stories.

_____

_____

_____

_____

4. As your child(ren) grow and mature, how will you measure success as a parent?

_____

_____

_____

_____

JOURNALING

1. Express the many ways you can convey respect, dignity, and love to your strong-willed adolescent.

_____

_____

_____

_____

2. Confess how you've at times shut down conversation with your child, and write out a three-point action plan for getting back into your child's life in a positive way.

_____

_____

_____

_____

3. Write a letter you'd like to give to your child when he or she leaves home. Express your love for him or her and words of encouragement for the future.

_____

_____

_____

_____

4. Think about ways you have held your child close (too close perhaps) over the years. Reflect on how the roles will shift when you have an empty nest.

_____

_____

_____

5. What are some of the things you'd like to see your adolescent busy with? How can you encourage him or her to get more involved with what matters most—with what matters for eternity?

_____

_____

_____

6. What are your greatest fears and joys when it comes to parenting a strong-willed adolescent? Spend time in prayer for your child, your spouse (if applicable), and yourself.

_____

_____

_____

APPENDIX

DEALING WITH THE ADHD CHILD

Taken from chapter 11, "Dealing with the ADHD Child"

Some strong-willed children also happen to have a condition known as attention deficit/hyperactivity disorder, or ADHD. Any physical problem that increases the level of activity and reduces self-control in a youngster is almost certain to create management problems. It is worse when that boy or girl is also inclined to resist parental authority. The connection between hyperactivity and defiance has been documented clinically.

The conjunction of those characteristics is likely to make life difficult, and in some cases, highly stressful for the mother, father, siblings, and teachers. Kids with the disorder frequently have few friends. Their parents may be ostracized by neighbors and relatives, who blame them for failing to control the child.

The *Journal of the American Medical Association* (*JAMA*) stated that ADHD "is among the most common neurodevelopmental disorders in children." The *British Medical Journal* estimated that approximately 7 percent of school-age children have ADHD, and that boys are affected three times as often as girls. A 1995 Virginia study showed that 8 percent to 10 percent of young school children were taking medication for ADHD. ADHD affects more than the affected individual—the time and effort required to deal with ADHD can significantly disrupt the entire family.

In most families, the mother has the greatest emotional, relational, and spiritual risk in caring for an ADHD child. Although these children can be intensely loving, they can also turn on their moms in a second. They can be verbally or emotionally abusive to their parents, which can wound parents deeply. They can be wonderful one day and horrible the next—or they can change from hour to hour.

Moms of ADHD kids need to quickly give up the delusion that their homes will be immaculate or that every meal will be a joyous family affair. ADHD parents have to learn that they are not perfect and that they may need help. Not only can they be rejected and hurt by their child, but these parents also may have to face the rejection, hostility, or animosity of children, other adults, or neighbors.

The ADHD child is often physically aggressive and must be taught to convert physical aggression into verbal expression (a skill some adults need to learn!). He or she may be verbally abusive. Once again, learning how to teach your child to redirect this harmful behavior into constructive behavior is essential. Parents of ADHD kids quickly learn that they cannot force or coerce their kids to be like "normal" kids—many of them will never adhere to that ideal. ADHD children are wired differently, and their parents need to learn a wide variety of parenting skills to cope with, teach, train, and creatively discipline these unique kids.

Let's not forget the siblings. They also have to live with the ADHD child, who can make life miserable for his unaffected brothers and sisters. Medical studies are beginning to show that siblings can also be at risk for emotional problems. These siblings can be chronically victimized by the ADHD child, who may bully them verbally or physically abuse them, and may be intense, demanding, and obnoxious.

Further, if siblings do not receive the attention and time that they need and deserve—because of the time and effort diverted to the ADHD child—they may feel alienated, rejected, or unloved. These feelings can lead to a range of behavioral problems, especially in adolescence. Therefore, many ADHD care providers recommend that siblings be part of the family counseling. The good news is that the skills these siblings gain will be helpful to them for life.

In *Driven to Distraction,* psychiatrists Edward M. Hallowell and John J. Ratey list twenty symptoms often seen in a person with ADHD. These are among the criteria used by doctors to make the diagnosis:

1. A sense of underachievement, of not meeting one's goals (regardless of how much one has accomplished)
2. Difficulty getting organized
3. Chronic procrastination or trouble getting started
4. Many projects going simultaneously; trouble with follow-through
5. Tendency to say what comes to mind without necessarily considering the timing or appropriateness of the remark
6. Ongoing search for high stimulation
7. Tendency to be easily bored

8. Easy distractibility, trouble focusing attention, tendency to tune out or drift away in the middle of a page or a conversation, often coupled with an ability to focus at times

9. Often creative, intuitive, highly intelligent

10. Trouble going through established channels, following proper procedure

11. Impatient; low tolerance for frustration

12. Impulsive, either verbally or in action, as in impulsive spending of money, changing plans, enacting new schemes or career plans, and the like

13. Tendency to worry needlessly, endlessly; tendency to scan the horizon looking for something to worry about alternating with inattention to or disregard for actual dangers

14. Sense of impending doom, insecurity, alternating with high risk-taking

15. Depression, especially when disengaged from a project

16. Restlessness

17. Tendency toward addictive behavior

18. Chronic problems with self-esteem

19. Inaccurate self-observation

20. Family history of ADD, manic-depressive illness, depression, substance abuse, or other disorders of impulse control or mood

For further information please refer to *The New Strong-Willed Child* or consult your family practitioner or pediatrician. This information is provided as a service to parents but should not be considered a substitute for obtaining a professional medical opinion about your child's individual situation.